Grade 8 Student Book

Accessing Complex Texts

- Annotate
- Collaborate
- Think About Text

Douglas Fisher • Nancy Frey

Table of Contents

Unit 1 Facing Challenges.....5

Passage 1 **Elizabeth Takes the Reins**
an excerpt from Understood Betsy
by Dorothy Canfield Fisher
Fiction

Passage 2 **The Necklace**
adapted from Guy de Maupassant's short story
Short Story

Passage 3 **Playing Pilgrims**
an excerpt from Chapter 1 of Little Women
by Louisa May Alcott
Realistic Fiction

Unit 2 Genes & Heredity....31

Passage 1 **Mendel's Discovery**
by Ted Kestral
Informational Text: Science

Passage 2 **Fancy Feather Gene**
by Stephen Ornes
News Article

Passage 3 **What's On Your Genes?**
by Sharon Pochron
News Article

Unit 3 The Constitution.....59

Passage 1 **Letters from the Convention**
Primary Source/Letters

Passage 2 **The Constitutional Convention Begins**
by Roger Bruns
Informational Text: Social Studies

Passage 3 **Benjamin Franklin's Speech**
at the Constitutional Convention
by Benjamin Franklin
Primary Source/Speech

Unit 4 Transformation......85

Passage 1 The Myth of Pygmalion
Myth

Passage 2 Operation Sherry
Realistic Fiction

Passage 3 Pygmalion
by George Bernard Shaw
Drama

Unit 5 The Civil War.......111

Passage 1 The Great Emancipator
by Harold Holzer
Historical Essay

Passage 2 O Captain! My Captain!
by Walt Whitman
Poem

Passage 3 The Civil War President
by Harold Holzer
Historical Essay

Unit 6 Space Frontiers......137

Passage 1 The Voyager Mission
Informational Text: Science

Passage 2 Great Achievements in Planetary Exploration
by Michelle Thaller
Personal Essay /Opinion

Passage 3 The Search for Another Earth
Informational Text: Science

Unit 1
Facing Challenges

Table of Contents
Elizabeth Takes the Reins 6
The Necklace 12
Playing Pilgrims 20

Remember to annotate as you read.

Notes

Passage 1

Unit 1 • Facing Challenges

Elizabeth Takes the Reins

an excerpt from *Understood Betsy*
by Dorothy Canfield Fisher

1   You can imagine, perhaps, the dreadful terror of Elizabeth Ann as the train carried her along toward Vermont and the horrible Putney Farm! It had happened so quickly—her satchel packed, the telegram sent, the train caught—that she had not had time to get her wits together, assert herself, and say that she would not go there! Besides, she had a sinking notion that perhaps they wouldn't pay any attention to her if she did. The world had come to an end now that Aunt Frances wasn't there to take care of her! And now she was not even being taken to Putney Farm! She was being sent!

2   Poor Elizabeth Ann's knees knocked against each other with fear of the strange faces she was to encounter. When the conductor came to help her get off, he had to carry the trembling child as well as her satchel. But there was only one strange face there. A grim-faced old man in a fur cap and heavy coat stood by a lumber wagon.

3   There was Elizabeth Ann alone with her much-feared Great-uncle Henry. He lifted her high to the seat, tossed her satchel into the wagon, climbed up himself, and clucked to his horses.

4   She sat very still on the high lumber seat, feeling very forlorn and neglected. She looked up at Uncle Henry with the wild eyes of nervous terror, which always brought Aunt Frances to her in a rush to "hear all about it."

5   Uncle Henry looked down at her soberly, his hard, weather-beaten old face quite unmoved. "Here, you drive, will you, for a piece?" he said briefly, putting the reins into her hands. "I've got some figgering to do. You pull on the left-hand rein to make 'em go to the left and t'other way for t'other way."

Accessing Complex Texts Now! • Grade 8 • © Benchmark Education Company, LLC

6   Elizabeth Ann had been so near one of her wild screams of terror that now, in spite of her instant interest in the reins, she gave a queer little yelp. She was all ready with the explanation. Her conversations with Aunt Frances having made her very fluent in explanations of her own emotions. But Uncle Henry seemed not to have heard her little howl. Or he didn't think it worth conversation, for he . . . Oh, the horses were certainly going to one side! She hastily decided which was her right hand and pulled furiously on that rein. The horses turned their heads a little, and, miraculously, there they were in the middle of the road again.

7   Elizabeth Ann drew a long breath of relief and pride, and looked to Uncle Henry for praise. But he had not noticed. Oh, they were going to the left again! This time she made a mistake about which hand was which and pulled wildly on the left line. The horses docilely walked off the road into a shallow ditch. Why didn't Uncle Henry help?

8   Elizabeth Ann, the perspiration starting out on her forehead, pulled on the other line. The horses turned back up the little slope. She was sure they would tip over! But somehow there they were in the road, safe and sound. But she must think of some way to avoid that hideous mistake again.

9   And then suddenly something inside Elizabeth Ann's head stirred and moved. It came to her, like a clap. She needn't know which was right or left at all if she just pulled the way she wanted them to go.

10 It was possible that what stirred inside her head at that moment was her brain, waking up. She was nine years old, but that was the first time she had ever had a whole thought of her very own. Somebody had always been explaining things to Elizabeth Ann so industriously that she had never found out a single thing for herself before. This was a very small discovery, but an original one. Elizabeth Ann was as excited about it as a mother-bird over the first egg that hatches.

Elizabeth Takes the Reins — Unit 1 • **Facing Challenges**

Close Reading and Collaborative Conversations

What Does the Text Say?	How Does the Text Work?
1. What is this passage mostly about? Turn to a partner and summarize "Elizabeth Takes the Reins."	**1.** The author uses many exclamation points and phrases with strong connotations in paragraph 1. How does this help the reader understand Elizabeth Ann's state of mind?
2. Why is Elizabeth Ann filled with "dreadful terror" at the beginning of the story? Use details from the text to support your answer.	**2.** What information can be gained from the description of Uncle Henry's behavior? How does it change the way the reader sees Elizabeth Ann?
3. At the end of the story, what is Elizabeth Ann excited about?	**3.** Reread paragraph 4. How does the author's description let the reader know more about how Elizabeth Ann was raised?

Unit 1 • Facing Challenges   Elizabeth Takes the Reins

What Does the Text Mean?

1. In paragraph 10, the author says that it "was possible that what stirred inside her head at that moment was her brain, waking up." What in this story so far gives the reader the impression that Elizabeth Ann's brain has been "asleep"?

2. This story is an excerpt from a novel. Based on what you've read so far about Elizabeth Ann, what clues are there about how her character will continue to develop?

3. In this passage, what does the author imply about Elizabeth Ann's feelings and behavior? Use details from the text to support your answer.

Elizabeth Takes the Reins Unit 1 • Facing Challenges

# Write About the Text

Argument Writing Prompt

Is the character Elizabeth Ann presented sympathetically or unsympathetically? After reading "Elizabeth Takes the Reins," write an essay defending your claim. Support your discussion with evidence from the text.

Plan your response using this graphic organizer. Use your annotations and your notes on pages 6–9 to find evidence for your essay.

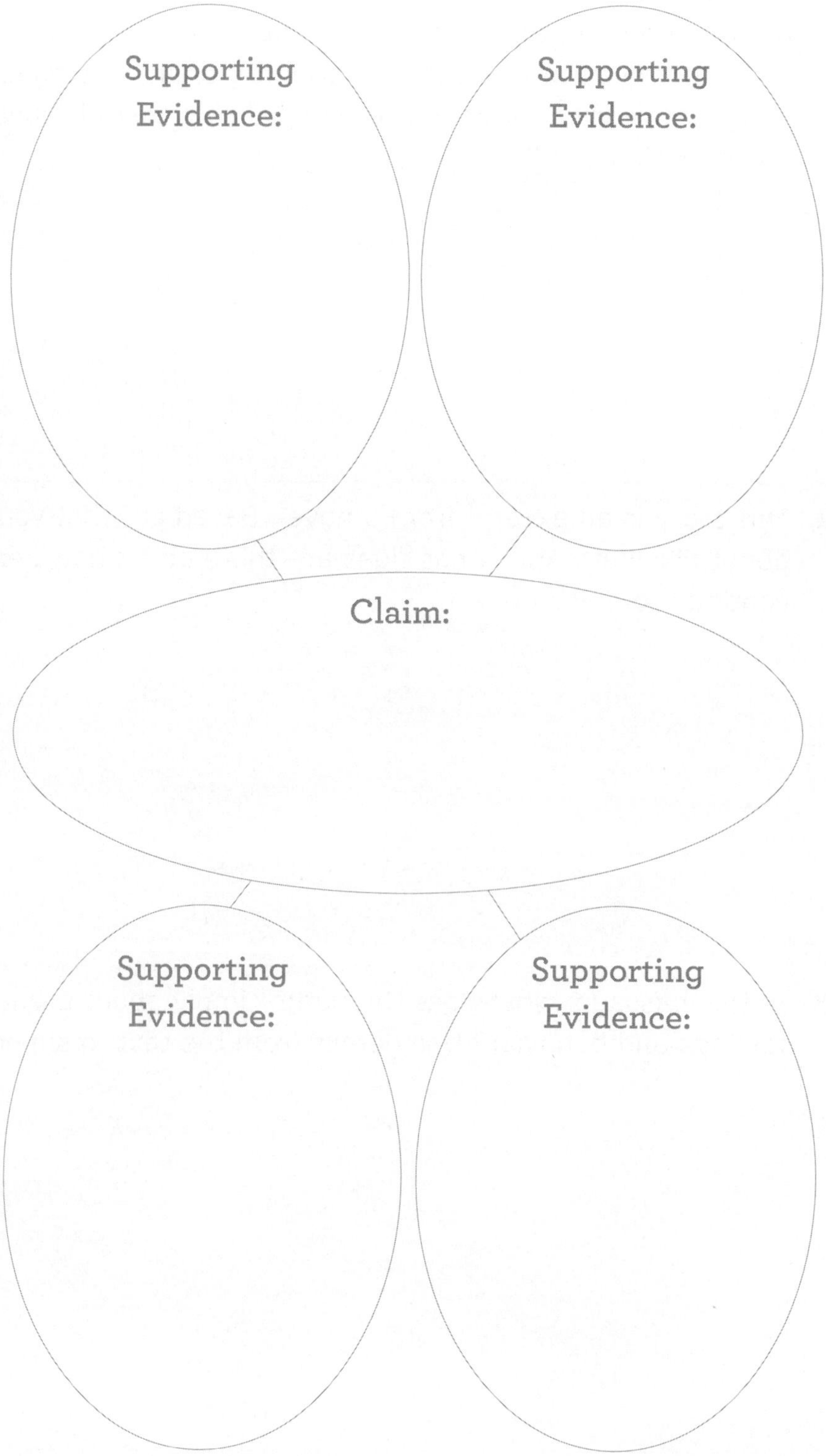

Supporting Evidence:

Supporting Evidence:

Claim:

Supporting Evidence:

Supporting Evidence:

Writer's Checklist

❏ I introduced the topic and clearly stated my claim.

❏ I acknowledged opposing claims.

❏ I supported my claim with evidence and logical reasoning.

❏ I used transitions to clarify the connections between ideas.

❏ I used a formal style.

❏ I have a concluding statement.

10 Accessing Complex Texts Now! • Grade 8 • © Benchmark Education Company, LLC

Unit 1 • Facing Challenges — Elizabeth Takes the Reins

Wrap Up
Check Your Understanding

1. Why does the author emphasize that Elizabeth Ann wasn't "being taken" to Putney Farm, but rather "she was being sent"?

   A. to show how cruelly Elizabeth Ann had been treated by her relatives

   B. to emphasize Elizabeth Ann's sense of helplessness

   C. to explain why Elizabeth Ann was so excited to meet Uncle Henry

   D. to illustrate how confused Elizabeth Ann was

2. This question has two parts. Answer Part A first, then answer Part B.

   Part A Why is Uncle Henry's advice about using the reins somewhat difficult for Elizabeth Ann to follow?

   A. She is too scared of horses to drive them.

   B. She is thinking about Aunt Frances too much to pay attention.

   C. She has a hard time telling her left from her right.

   D. She is too distracted by Uncle Henry's expression to listen carefully.

   Part B What evidence in the text supports the answer you chose?

   A. "Elizabeth Ann had been so near one of her wild screams of terror . . ."

   B. "Her conversations with Aunt Frances having made her very fluent in explanations of her own emotions."

   C. "Elizabeth Ann drew a long breath of relief and pride, and looked to Uncle Henry for praise."

   D. "This time she made a mistake about which hand was which and pulled wildly on the left line."

Remember to annotate as you read.

Notes

Passage 2

Unit 1 • Facing Challenges

The Necklace

Adapted from Guy de Maupassant's short story, "The Necklace"

1   Mathilde Loisel was one of those pretty and charming girls, but she let herself be married off to a little clerk in the Ministry of Education. She was unhappy as though she had married beneath her. She suffered endlessly, feeling herself born for every delicacy and luxury. She suffered from the poorness of her house, from its worn chairs and ugly curtains. She imagined vast saloons hung with antique silks, exquisite pieces of furniture supporting priceless ornaments, and small, charming, perfumed rooms, created just for little parties of intimate friends.

2   She had no clothes, no jewels, nothing. And these were the only things she loved; she felt that she was made for them. She had longed so eagerly to charm, to be desired, to be wildly attractive and sought after.

3   Mathilde had a rich friend, an old school chum whom she refused to visit, because she suffered so keenly when she returned home. One evening her husband came home with an exultant air, holding a large envelope in his hand. It was an invitation to a party, but instead of being delighted, as her husband hoped, she flung the invitation petulantly across the table. When asked what the matter was, she explained that she did not own a suitable dress.

4   Her husband gave her all the money he had in his wallet and Mathilde bought a new dress, but still she was upset. When her husband asked what was wrong, she replied, "I'm utterly miserable at not having any jewels, not a single stone, to wear. I would almost rather not go to the party."

12   Accessing Complex Texts Now! • Grade 8 • © Benchmark Education Company, LLC

5   When her husband suggested that she wear flowers, she told him that "there was nothing so humiliating as looking poor in the middle of a lot of rich women."

6   Finally, her husband told her to visit her rich friend and ask to borrow a necklace. With that, Madame Loisel uttered a cry of delight.

7   The next day she went to see her friend and, sure enough, Madame Forestier took up a large box and handed it to her friend, Mathilde. She told Mathilde that she was welcome to borrow anything she liked.

8   Mathilde discovered, in a black satin case, a superb diamond necklace; her heart began to beat covetously. Her hands trembled as she lifted it. She fastened it round her neck, upon her high dress, and remained in ecstasy at the sight of herself.

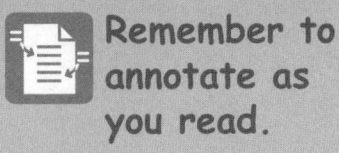

Notes

9   At the party, Mathilde was the prettiest woman present, elegant, graceful, smiling, and quite above herself with happiness. All the men stared at her and asked to be introduced to her.

10 When they arrived home from the party, Mathilde took off all her garments, so as to see herself in all her glory before the mirror. But suddenly she uttered a cry. The necklace was no longer round her neck!

11 When her husband understood what she was trying to say, they stared at one another, dumbfounded. At last, her husband went out to search for the necklace.

12 After a week of searching, they had lost all hope. In a shop they found a string of diamonds which seemed exactly like the one they had lost. Her husband borrowed from a whole tribe of money lenders to pay for the replacement.

13 When Mathilde returned the necklace, she did not tell her friend about how she had lost it. Madame Forestier said in a chilly voice, "You ought to have brought it back sooner; I might have needed it." Mathilde only nodded.

14 Mathilde came to know the ghastly life of abject poverty; the heavy work of the house, the hateful duties

of the kitchen. And, clad like a poor woman, she went to the grocer, to the butcher, haggling, fighting for every wretched halfpenny of her money.

15   And this life lasted ten years.

16   One Sunday, as she had gone for a walk, Mathilde spotted Madame Forestier, who was still young and beautiful.

17   Mathilde approached Madame Forestier, but she did not recognize her.

18   "I am Mathilde Loisel," she said.

19   Her friend uttered a cry.

20   Mathilde told Madame Forestier that she had come upon hard times and many sorrows. She told her that she and her husband had spent a decade paying back the debt for the diamond necklace that she borrowed and lost.

21   Madame Forestier listened, and then she said, "Oh, my poor Mathilde, my necklace was imitation."

The Necklace — Unit 1 • Facing Challenges

Close Reading and Collaborative Conversations

What Does the Text Say?	How Does the Text Work?
1. What is the story mostly about? Turn to a partner and summarize "The Necklace."	**1.** In paragraph 2, what does the author mean when he says Mathilde has "no clothes, no jewels, nothing"? Use evidence from the text to support your answer.
2. Why does Mathilde at first not want to go to the party? Why does she change her mind? Use evidence from the text to support your answer.	**2.** Mathilde no longer loves her husband. How does her husband feel about her? How does the author reveal the husband's feelings?
3. How do Mathilde and her husband react differently to realizing that the necklace is lost, and what do these actions say about their characters?	**3.** What is the author's point of view of the character Mathilde? Use details from the text to support your ideas.

Unit 1 • FACING CHALLENGES   The Necklace

What Does the Text Mean?

1. Poetic justice is a literary term meaning that a character "gets what he or she deserves." How has Mathilde experienced poetic justice in this story? Use evidence from the story in your answer.

2. Mathilde is clearly not an admirable character. What about her husband? What character weaknesses does he display in the text? How does the author feel about him?

3. What lesson has Mathilde learned at the end of the story? How can the reader see that she has learned this lesson?

The Necklace | Unit 1 • Facing Challenges

# Write About the Text

Informative/Explanatory Writing Prompt

After reading "The Necklace," write an essay explaining how Mathilde's desire for luxury actually results in her becoming even poorer. Support your discussion with evidence from the text.

Plan your response using this graphic organizer. Use your annotations and your notes on pages 12–17 to find evidence for your essay.

Introduction:

Example:

Supporting Text Evidence:

Example:

Supporting Text Evidence:

Conclusion:

Writer's Checklist

- ❏ I introduced the topic.
- ❏ I clearly organized my ideas.
- ❏ I developed the topic with facts, details, and evidence.
- ❏ I used transitions to connect ideas.
- ❏ I used precise language.
- ❏ I used a formal style.
- ❏ I included a concluding statement.

Unit 1 • Facing Challenges   The Necklace

Wrap Up
Check Your Understanding

1. In paragraph 1, the author says that Mathilde "let herself be married off" to her husband. What does this say about how Mathilde sees her circumstances?

    A. She doesn't take responsibility for her choice of husband.

    B. She was once very wealthy but is no longer wealthy.

    C. She was forced to marry her husband.

    D. She didn't have any other marriage prospects.

2. This question has two parts. Answer Part A first, then answer Part B.

    Part A What word best explains Madame Forestier's reaction to seeing Mathilde at the end of the story?

    A. happy

    B. surprised

    C. embarrassed

    D. sad

    Part B What evidence in the text supports the answer you chose?

    A. "Oh, my poor Mathilde . . ."

    B. ". . . my necklace was imitation."

    C. ". . . but she did not recognize her."

    D. "Her friend uttered a cry."

© Benchmark Education Company, LLC • Grade 8 • Accessing Complex Texts Now!   19

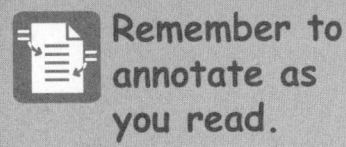

Passage 3 — Unit 1 • Facing Challenges

Playing Pilgrims

An excerpt from Chapter 1 of *Little Women*

by LOUISA MAY ALCOTT

1   "Christmas won't be Christmas without any presents," grumbled Jo, lying on the rug.

2   "It's so dreadful to be poor!" sighed Meg, looking down at her old dress.

3   "I don't think it's fair for some girls to have plenty of pretty things, and other girls nothing at all," added little Amy, with an injured sniff.

4   "We've got Father and Mother, and each other," said Beth contentedly from her corner.

5   The four young faces on which the firelight shone brightened at the cheerful words, but darkened again as Jo said sadly, "We haven't got Father, and shall not have him for a long time." She didn't say "perhaps never," but each silently added it, thinking of Father far away, where the fighting was.

6   Nobody spoke for a minute; then Meg said in an altered tone, "You know the reason Mother proposed not having any presents this Christmas was because it is going to be a hard winter for everyone; and she thinks we ought not to spend money for pleasure, when our men are suffering so in the army. We can't do much, but we can make our little sacrifices, and ought to do it gladly. But I am afraid I don't," and Meg shook her head, as she thought regretfully of all the pretty things she wanted.

7   "But I don't think the little we should spend would do any good. We've each got a dollar, and the army wouldn't be much helped by our giving that. I agree not to expect anything from Mother or you, but I do want to buy *Undine and Sintram* for myself. I've wanted it so long," said Jo, who was a bookworm.

8   "I planned to spend mine in new music," said Beth, with a little sigh, which no one heard but the hearth brush and kettle-holder.

9   "I shall get a nice box of Faber's drawing pencils; I really need them," said Amy decidedly.

10 "Mother didn't say anything about our money, and she won't wish us to give up everything. Let's each buy what we want, and have a little fun; I'm sure we work hard enough to earn it," cried Jo, examining the heels of her shoes in a gentlemanly manner.

11 "I know I do—teaching those tiresome children nearly all day, when I'm longing to enjoy myself at home," began Meg, in the complaining tone again.

12 "You don't have half such a hard time as I do," said Jo. "How would you like to be shut up for hours with a nervous, fussy old lady, who keeps you trotting, is never satisfied, and worries you till you're ready to fly out the window or cry?"

13 "It's naughty to fret, but I do think washing dishes and keeping things tidy is the worst work in the world. It makes me cross, and my hands get so stiff, I can't practice well at all." And Beth looked at her rough hands with a sigh that any one could hear that time.

14 "I don't believe any of you suffer as I do," cried Amy, "for you don't have to go to school with impolite girls, who laugh at your dresses, and label your father if he isn't rich, and insult you when your nose isn't nice."

15 "Don't peck at one another, children. Don't you wish we had the money Papa lost when we were little, Jo? Dear me! How happy and good we'd be, if we had no worries!" said Meg, who could remember better times.

16 "You said the other day you thought we were a deal happier than the King children, for they were fighting and fretting all the time, in spite of their money."

17 "So I did, Beth. Well, I think we are. For though we do have to work, we make fun of ourselves, and are a pretty jolly set, as Jo would say."

18 "Jo does use such slang words!" observed Amy.

19 Jo immediately sat up, put her hands in her pockets, and began to whistle.

20 "Don't, Jo. It's so boyish!"

21 "That's why I do it."

22 "I detest rude, unladylike girls!"

23 "I hate affected, niminy-piminy chits!"

24 "Birds in their little nests agree," sang Beth, the peacemaker, with such a funny face that both sharp voices softened to a laugh, and the "pecking" ended for that time.

25 "Really, girls, you are both to be blamed," said Meg, beginning to lecture in her elder-sisterly fashion. "You are old enough to leave off boyish tricks. You need to behave better, Josephine. It didn't matter so much when you were a little girl. But now you are so tall, and turn up your hair, you should remember that you are a young lady."

26 "I'm not! And if turning up my hair makes me one, I'll wear it in two tails till I'm twenty," cried Jo, pulling off her net, and shaking down a chestnut mane. "It's bad enough to be a girl, anyway, when I like boy's games and work and manners! I can't get over my disappointment in not being a boy. And it's worse than ever now, for I'm dying to go and fight with Papa. And I can only stay home and knit, like a poky old woman!"

27 And Jo shook the blue army sock till the needles rattled like castanets, and her ball bounded across the room.

28 "Poor Jo! It's too bad, but it can't be helped. So you must try to be contented with making your name boyish, and playing brother to us girls," said Beth, stroking the rough head with a hand that all the dish washing and dusting in the world could not make ungentle in its touch.

29 "As for you, Amy," continued Meg, "you are altogether too particular and prim. Your airs are funny now, but you'll grow up an affected little goose, if you don't take care. I like your nice manners and refined ways of speaking, when you don't try to be elegant. But your absurd words are as bad as Jo's slang."

30 "If Jo is a tomboy and Amy a goose, what am I, please?" asked Beth, ready to share the lecture.

31 "You're a dear, and nothing else," answered Meg warmly. No one contradicted her, for the "Mouse" was the pet of the family.

Playing Pilgrims — Unit 1 • **Facing Challenges**

Close Reading and Collaborative Conversations

What Does the Text Say?	How Does the Text Work?
1. What is the main problem the sisters face in "Playing Pilgrims"? Use evidence from the story as part of your answer.	**1.** What does the reader learn about Amy from the first statement she makes in this excerpt? What kind of person does the author reveal Amy to be?
2. What events led Mother to propose that the girls not receive gifts for Christmas?	**2.** How does the way Beth breaks up the argument between Jo and Amy show the reader what to think about Beth's character? Use details from the text to support your response.
3. Reread paragraphs 18–23. What does the reader learn about Jo and Amy's relationship in this section of the excerpt?	**3.** How does Jo feel about Meg calling her a "young lady"? What evidence from the text shows her point of view?

What Does the Text Mean?

1. Do the girls' personality differences seem typical of siblings, or is it odd that they are so different from one another? Compare these siblings to other siblings you may have read about or seen in a film.

2. How do the characters in this passage differ in their attitude toward being poor to the characters in "The Necklace"? Give evidence to support your answer.

3. What lesson is the author sharing about the nature of a sibling relationship in this passage? Use details from the text to support your answer.

Playing Pilgrims | Unit 1 • Facing Challenges

Write About the Text

Argument Writing Prompt

After reading "Playing Pilgrims," write an essay answering the question: Which of the four sisters has the most admirable personality traits? Support your argument with evidence from the text.

Plan your response using this graphic organizer. Use your annotations and your notes on pages 20–25 to find evidence for your essay.

Supporting Evidence:

Supporting Evidence:

Claim:

Supporting Evidence:

Supporting Evidence:

Writer's Checklist

- ❏ I introduced the topic and clearly stated my claim.
- ❏ I acknowledged opposing claims.
- ❏ I supported my claim with evidence and logical reasoning.
- ❏ I used transitions to clarify the connections between ideas.
- ❏ I used a formal style.
- ❏ I have a concluding statement.

Unit 1 • Facing Challenges   Playing Pilgrims

Wrap Up
Check Your Understanding

1. What is the author showing by writing in paragraph 8 that Beth spoke "with a little sigh, which no one heard but the hearth brush and kettle-holder"?

    A. Beth is quick to complain, enough so that her sisters now ignore her.

    B. Beth sighs so gently, that none of her sisters even hear her.

    C. Beth is responsible for taking care of the fireplace equipment.

    D. Beth is frightened to have her sisters hear her complain.

2. This question has two parts. Answer Part A first, then answer Part B.

    Part A What is Meg's role in the family? How does she relate to her sisters?

    A. She is the one they all seem to like the least.

    B. She feels that she can advise and judge each of them.

    C. She is the most beloved of all of the sisters.

    D. She wishes that she were a child again, without all of her siblings.

    Part B What evidence in the text supports the answer you chose?

    A. "'It's so dreadful to be poor!' sighed Meg, looking down at her old dress."

    B. "We can't do much, but we can make our little sacrifices, and ought to do it gladly."

    C. "Don't you wish we had the money Papa lost when we were little, Jo?"

    D. "'You're a dear, and nothing else,' answered Meg warmly."

© Benchmark Education Company, LLC • Grade 8 • Accessing Complex Texts Now!   27

Playing Pilgrims   Unit 1 • Facing Challenges

 # Wrap Up
Check Your Understanding

3. Which of the following words or phrases describes the character of Jo? Check the box next to each correct answer.
   - ☐ shy
   - ☐ interested in drawing
   - ☐ motherly
   - ☐ opinionated
   - ☐ interested in reading
   - ☐ sickly

4. Which theme do "Playing Pilgrims" and "The Necklace" have in common?
    - **A.** Being poor can be difficult.
    - **B.** Love conquers all.
    - **C.** Sisters can be best friends.
    - **D.** Vanity can be the downfall of a person.

Unit 1 • Facing Challenges   Read and Write Across Texts

# Read and Write Across Texts

Plan your response using this graphic organizer.
Use your annotations and the notes you've taken on each passage to identify supporting evidence for your essay.

Introduction:

Evidence from "Elizabeth Takes the Reins":

Informative/Explanatory Writing Prompt

Each text focuses on characters who want something they don't have. How do the authors of each passage show that the characters will or won't get what they want? Write an essay addressing this question. Support your position with examples from the texts.

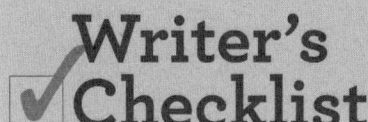

Writer's ✓Checklist

❑ I introduced the topic.
❑ I clearly organized my ideas.
❑ I developed the topic with facts, details, and evidence.
❑ I used transitions to connect ideas.
❑ I used precise language.
❑ I used a formal style.
❑ I included a concluding statement.

© Benchmark Education Company, LLC • Grade 8 • Accessing Complex Texts Now!

Evidence from "The Necklace":

Evidence from "Playing Pilgrims":

Conclusion:

Unit 2
Genes & Heredity

Table of Contents
Mendel's Discovery 32
Fancy Feather Gene 40
What's On Your Genes? 46

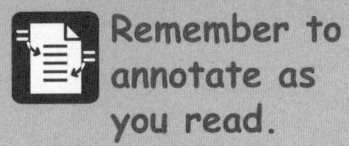

Notes

Mendel's Discovery

By Ted Kestral

1   Why do so many people look like their parents and other relatives? For that matter, why do elephants always give birth to elephants, instead of giving birth to frogs or cows? How come each of us has some traits, or distinguishing characteristics, that don't seem to come from either parent?

2   It wasn't until the late 1800s that scientists began to understand how inheritance worked. This was the result of the work of a monk named Gregor Mendel. His research helped explain of how traits were passed from one generation to the next.

3   Before Mendel, the most popular theory among scientists was that inherited traits "blended" from generation to generation. This seemed to make sense. After all, when gardeners cross-bred a white carnation with a red carnation, they usually produced a pink one. So it was reasonable to believe that the plants' traits had simply "blended."

4   For his research, Mendel did a series of experiments using pea plants. He chose pea plants for several reasons. They can be grown quickly. Their seeds have sharply contrasting characteristics. In addition, their reproduction can be easily manipulated with cross-pollination. Cross-pollination is the process of mixing the genetic material of two plants. Each pea plant has both male and female reproductive organs. They can reproduce either by self-pollinating or by cross-pollinating with another plant.

Unit 2 • Genes & Heredity   Mendel's Discovery

Gregor Mendel (1822–1884) created a revolutionary shift in understanding of how traits are passed on from one generation to the next through his pea plant experiments.

Notes

5   Mendel focused on just a few specific traits in order to get clear, simple results. He identified seven simple traits in pea plants that occurred only in one of two different forms. In other words, they never "blended." For instance, flower color in pea plants could be purple or white. But it was never lavender, a mix of the two. Stem length could be long or short but not in between. Seed color could be yellow or green but not yellowish green.

6   Mendel noticed that plants that reproduced by self-pollination always had offspring identical to themselves. Plants that reproduced by cross-pollination did not. Mendel carefully cross-pollinated "purebred" plants that had contrasting traits. After observing the outcome over several generations. Mendel came to some conclusions that changed how people thought traits were passed from generation to generation.

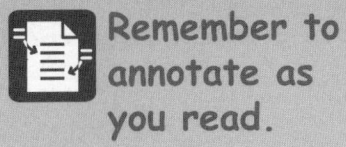

Remember to annotate as you read.

Notes

Passage 1
continued

Unit 2 • Genes & Heredity

7   Mendel started using "parent" plants whose genetic background was known. He discovered that when he crossed pure yellow-seeded plants-that is, yellow-seeded plants that descended from plants that produced only yellow seeds-with pure green-seeded plants, the cross-pollination yielded offspring that had only yellow seeds. The green color seemed to have vanished entirely. However, when he allowed these yellow-seeded plants to self-pollinate, plants with some green seeds reappeared in the next generation. Even more intriguing, this occurred in a consistent ratio. There would be three yellow seeds for each green one.

Mendel used pea plants with distinct traits, such as flower color, to get clear, simple results.

Unit 2 • Genes & Heredity — Mendel's Discovery

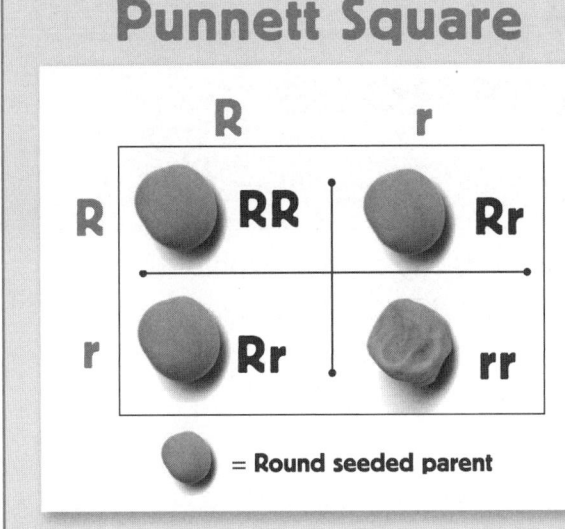

Punnett Square

This diagram, called a Punnett square, shows the way traits can be passed on with a pairing of traits. In this case, plants with round seeds and plants with crinkled seeds.

= Round seeded parent

Notes

8   So where did the trait for green seeds "go" in that first generation of yellow-seeded plants? And why did they reappear at such a regular ratio in later generations? Mendel drew three important conclusions:

9   1. The inheritance of each trait is determined by "a pair of units" (which we now call genes) that are passed unchanged to the next generation.

10 2. Reproducing parents produce sex cells and in the formation of these, one member of each pair of genes (now called an allele) moves into a separate sex cell. An individual receives one such "unit" from each parent, for each trait.

11 3. Even though a trait may not be visible in an individual, the trait can still be passed on to the next generation. When plants without contrasting traits, such as yellow seeds and green seeds, are crossed, if only one of the traits appears in the offspring, it is called the dominant trait. The trait not seen in the offspring is called the recessive trait.

12 This is known as Mendel's law of dominance.

Mendel's Discovery | Unit 2 • Genes & Heredity

Close Reading and Collaborative Conversations

What Does the Text Say?	How Does the Text Work?
1. What is the main of idea of "Mendel's Discovery"? Turn to a partner and summarize the text.	**1.** Why does the author explain the point of view of scientists who came before Mendel in paragraph 3? How does the author respond to the conflicting viewpoint?
2. Reread paragraph 6. What is the main difference between the results of self-pollination and cross-pollination? Why was cross-pollination important in Mendel's experiments?	**2.** What is the purpose of paragraph 5, and how does the author construct the paragraph to get his point across?
3. How do dominant and recessive genes interact when passed down through generations?	**3.** Reread paragraphs 4 through 7. What is "self-pollination"? Why was it an important part of Mendel's experiments?

Unit 2 • Genes & Heredity   Mendel's Discovery

What Does the Text Mean?
1. How does the author show that Mendel was personally credited with a new discovery? What does the author do to demonstrate Mendel's importance to the history of genetic science?
2. Does the author adequately explain how traits for which there were more than two expressions could be predicted in future generations, for example a blue-eyed woman and a brown-eyed man can produce a child with hazel eyes? Explain whether or not the text adequately analyzes this concept.
3. How does the information in the article help you understand human genetic traits that are binary (only two options), such as connected earlobes or notched earlobes?

Mendel's Discovery | Unit 2 • Genes & Heredity

Write About the Text

Informative/Explanatory Writing Prompt

After reading "Mendel's Discovery," write an essay explaining the main ideas about how dominant and recessive genes interact in offspring. Support your discussion with evidence from the text.

Plan your response using this graphic organizer. Use your annotations and your notes on pages 32–37 to find evidence for your essay.

Introduction:

Example:

Supporting Text Evidence:

Example:

Supporting Text Evidence:

Conclusion:

Writer's Checklist

- ❏ I introduced the topic.
- ❏ I clearly organized my ideas.
- ❏ I developed the topic with facts, details, and evidence.
- ❏ I used transitions to connect ideas.
- ❏ I used precise language.
- ❏ I used a formal style.
- ❏ I included a concluding statement.

Wrap Up
Check Your Understanding

1. This question has two parts. Answer Part A first. Then answer Part B.

   Part A What is one reason why Mendel used pea plants for his experiments?

   A. They had many blended traits.

   B. The seeds have traits that appear very different to the naked eye.

   C. They have a very long lifespan.

   D. They almost never cross-pollinate.

   Part B What evidence in the text supports the answer you chose?

   A. "Each pea plant has both male and female reproductive organs."

   B. "They can reproduce either by self-pollinating or by cross-pollinating with another plant."

   C. "They can be grown quickly."

   D. "Their seeds have sharply contrasting characteristics."

2. What does the author mean in the second-to-last sentence of paragraph 7 by the term consistent ratio?

   A. predicable amount of each trait

   B. steady volume

   C. surprising amount

   D. complimentary colors

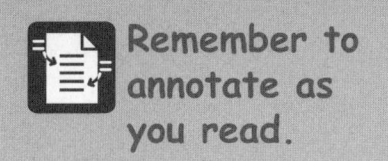

Fancy Feather Gene

A tweak in a single pigeon gene causes a distinct feather formation

BY STEPHEN ORNES

1   What a difference a gene makes! For pigeons, one gene can make or break the appearance of fancy feathers.

2   Many pigeons have crests or collars, tufts of feathers on the head or neck that appear to go the wrong way. They point up toward the head instead of down toward the tail. This funny feature decorates many different pigeon breeds, but all of those birds have one thing in common: A genetic alteration. In January, scientists reported they had pinpointed the altered gene responsible for the feathery twist.

3   A gene is a tiny segment of DNA. DNA's long, ladder-like molecule is found inside nearly every cell of every organism. Genes instruct a cell on how to function. Within individuals of the same species, most genes will be the same. But some genes may show slight differences, called mutations. In humans, blue eyes are the result of a genetic mutation. Mutations can develop naturally (think of some as a copying mistake) and then will be passed down from parents to their offspring.

4   Previous studies have suggested that a single genetic mutation is responsible for the funny feathers. But no one had found it. So biologist Michael Shapiro of the University of Utah in Salt Lake City and his coworkers went scouting for it. His team first gathered DNA from the cells of rock pigeons with the wrong-way feathers. Then the researchers gathered DNA from rock pigeons without crests or collars.

Unit 2 • Genes & Heredity   Fancy Feather Gene

Pigeons with crests of feathers are an example of a gene mutation.

5   The researchers compared the DNA from both types of birds. They found a mutation of a single gene, called *EphB2*, in pigeons with crests or collars. Birds with straight feathers lacked the mutation. So it alone seems to explain the strange plumage in some pigeons.

6   "This mutation that we found appears to be the on/off switch for crest development," Shapiro told *Science News*.

7   The researchers say the mutation probably arose naturally a long time ago in one breed of rock pigeon. Later, it likely spread to other breeds as crested birds bred with those without crests. (Like dogs, different breeds of rock pigeons can look very different from one another, but all belong to the same species.)

8   The new finding suggests major physical differences in other species may also trace to one or more tweaked genes, says Scott Edwards. This Harvard University biologist, who specializes in birds, did not participate in the new study.

9   Other species of birds also have crests, but Shapiro's team doesn't yet know if they are due to the same mutation.

Notes

Fancy Feather Gene   Unit 2 • Genes & Heredity

Close Reading and Collaborative Conversations

What Does the Text Say?	How Does the Text Work?
1. What is the central idea of "Fancy Feather Gene"? Turn to a partner and summarize the text.	1. What does the author mean by using the phrase "make or break" in the second sentence of this article? Explain in scientific terms what he is describing.
2. How does the author compare human mutation and pigeon mutation? Use details from the text to support your answer.	2. Why does the author choose to end the article with the concept he shares in the last paragraph? How is that a fitting end to the article?
3. What news is this article reporting? When was the news reported, what was the news, and who was the main person reported on?	3. In paragraph 7, why is the information in parentheses presented in that style? How does that information refine a key concept in the article?

What Does the Text Mean?

1. Both Mendel and the scientists who studied the wrong-way feathers in pigeons were testing a hypothesis. How were their hypotheses different and similar?

2. Did the author explain the evidence given that shows that the wrong-way feathers are a result of a single gene's mutation? Explain what the evidence is and whether or not it is convincing.

3. Why does the author use the phrase "seems to" and the scientist, Shapiro, uses the phrase "appears to be" when describing the conclusions about the expression of gene *EphB2*?

Fancy Feather Gene Unit 2 • Genes & Heredity

Write About the Text

Argument Writing Prompt

After reading "Fancy Feather Gene," write an essay answering the question: Are the findings of biologist Michael Shapiro convincing? Has he effectively proven that the gene *EphB2* controls the appearance of feathers that point the wrong way on pigeons? Support your opinion with evidence from the text.

Writer's Checklist

- ❏ I introduced the topic and stated my claim.
- ❏ I acknowledged opposing claims.
- ❏ I supported my claim with evidence and logical reasoning.
- ❏ I used transitions to make connections and clarify ideas.
- ❏ I used a formal style.
- ❏ I included a concluding statement.

Plan your response using this graphic organizer. Use your annotations and your notes on pages 40–43 to find evidence for your essay.

Supporting Evidence:

Supporting Evidence:

Claim:

Supporting Evidence:

Supporting Evidence:

44 Accessing Complex Texts Now! • Grade 8 • © Benchmark Education Company, LLC

Unit 2 • Genes & Heredity   Fancy Feather Gene?

Wrap Up
Check Your Understanding

1. In paragraph 4, what does the author mean when he states that the scientists went <u>scouting</u> for the single genetic mutation that controls the funny feathers?

    A. They wanted to publicize it.

    B. They went looking for it.

    C. They wanted to prove it didn't exist.

    D. They wanted to explain it.

2. This question has two parts. Answer Part A first. Then answer Part B.

    Part A What finding did Shapiro and his team discover during their research?

    A. that rock pigeons have a very different genetic structure than other pigeons

    B. that a single-gene mutation may be responsible for the difference in crested and uncrested pigeons

    C. that different breeds of rock pigeons can look very different from one another

    D. that mutations are a natural way that species develop

    Part B What evidence in the text supports the answer you chose?

    A. "But some genes may show slight differences, called mutations."

    B. "Like dogs, different breeds of rock pigeons can look very different from one another . . . "

    C. "They found a mutation of a single gene, called *EphB2*, in pigeons with crests or collars."

    D. "Mutations can develop naturally . . . "

Passage 3 — Unit 2 • Genes & Heredity

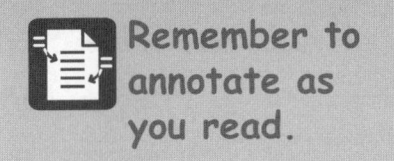

What's On Your Genes?

Tiny genetic switches create big differences • BY SHARON POCHRON

1   We've all heard it before: "It's in your genes."

2   If you're lucky, a parent or neighbor is trying to explain one of your good quirks, not one of your goofy ones. "Your father could hit the ball out of the park, too," someone might say. Or you have the same unruly curls as your mom. Thankfully, that someone hasn't heard you and your dad snore.

3   But what if it's not in your genes. What if it's on your genes?

4   In 1866, Gregor Mendel showed that pea plants inherit physical and other traits from their parents according to very precise laws of nature. In 1910, Thomas Hunt Morgan showed that genes exist on chromosomes, and in 1952 Martha Chase and Alfred Hershey showed that DNA within a gene carries traits from parent to child. When someone tells you, "It's in your genes," they're saying that the part of your chromosome responsible for your quirk matches that part of the chromosome on your equally quirky parent.

5   Except when it doesn't.

6   Imagine two mice. One looks normal. It's tiny and brown. The other is fat and has orange fur. The orange mouse not only looks weird, its weight makes it more prone to diabetes and cancer.

7   The biggest surprise isn't the differences between these mice—it's the similarities. The mice have the same DNA in the same order on the same chromosomes. They're genetically identical. The difference between the mice isn't in their genes; it's on them.

8   Methyl groups—chemical clusters each made of one carbon and three hydrogen atoms—latch onto DNA near a gene. Methyl groups act like switches, turning a gene on or off. In the case of the fat, orange mouse, scientist Randy Jirtle and his colleagues at Duke University used methyl groups to turn off something called the Agouti (a-goo-tee) gene. How? It was pretty simple.

9   In 2003, Jirtle fed pregnant mice a particular diet that turned off the Agouti gene in the mama mice's babies. The Agouti gene controls fur color and the feeling of fullness after eating. With the gene switched on, the baby mice grew into orange adults that could never eat enough to be satisfied. As a comparison, the scientists fed a vitamin-rich mouse diet to pregnant mice that were genetically identical to the first group. The Agouti gene was switched off in the babies of those moms who had eaten the vitamin-rich chow. Those pups developed brown fur and a feeling of fullness after eating.

When the Agouti gene is switched on, the baby mice grew into orange adults with big appetites.

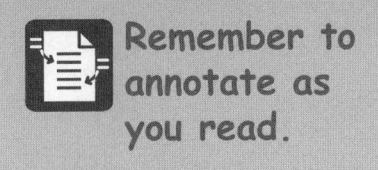

10 Same genes, different methyl patterns—very different looking mice. Without changing the DNA in the Agouti gene, Jirtle and his colleagues showed the power of what scientists call an epigenetic change.

11 "Epigenetic literally means 'above the genes,'" explains Jirtle. Epigenetic changes don't rewrite DNA, the genetic code. Instead, the activity of the genes is altered. Genes contain the recipe for proteins. Every time a gene is turned on, it makes its particular protein. But how much—if any—of the protein a gene makes and when it makes the protein can be altered by the addition or deletion of methyl groups.

12 In October 2010, Margaret Morris and her colleagues at the University of New South Wales in Sydney, Australia, took epigenetic research a step further. She showed that babies could inherit epigenetic changes—a scenario never before imagined by geneticists.

13 "We asked whether the diet of the father might affect his babies," Morris said.

14 She took a bunch of healthy, identical male rats and put half on a high-fat diet. The other half ate regular food. Males on high-fat diets became overweight and diabetic (a common complication of obesity in humans). Males on regular diets grew into normal rats. All males mated with genetically identical females who had been raised on a standard rodent diet. Later, Morris examined the daughters of these rats. Would the obese fathers' weight problems affect their offspring? Nothing learned from Mendel and his peas would make scientists expect that it would.

15 But Mendel and his peas don't tell us about epigenetics.

16 Morris found that none of the rat daughters developed a weight problem, which isn't surprising given what we know about standard genetics. However, daughters of fat dads did develop health problems related to obesity.

Methyl groups latch onto DNA strands. They can turn a gene on or off.

17 "Female baby rats looked as though they were on their way to becoming diabetic. They couldn't produce enough insulin," explains Morris.

18 Insulin is a hormone needed for the body to use glucose—also known as blood sugar. Glucose is the body's energy source. A shortage of insulin or the body's inability to use insulin effectively causes diabetes, a very serious disease.

19 Genetic changes clearly didn't cause the daughters' insulin problems, because the scientists had used genetically identical rats. Instead, fat dads created sperm cells with different methyl patterns on their DNA. Daughters inherited their father's epigenetic changes. And because of changes in methyl patterns on the genes, daughters also inherited their dads' health problems.

20 Foods that our parents eat before we're born or while we're still inside the womb can affect epigenetic switches. Smoking, drinking alcohol and aging can all cause epigenetic changes too.

21 But can behavior create epigenetic changes? Michael Meaney and his colleagues at McGill University in Montreal answered that question in 2004 with rats.

22 Some mother rats lick their babies a lot. Other mothers ignore their babies. Different kinds of mothering cause babies to become different kinds of adults. No one thinks adult rats remember whether their mothers licked them. But research has shown that licked babies grow up to be braver in the face of stress. Ignored babies are more scared as adults.

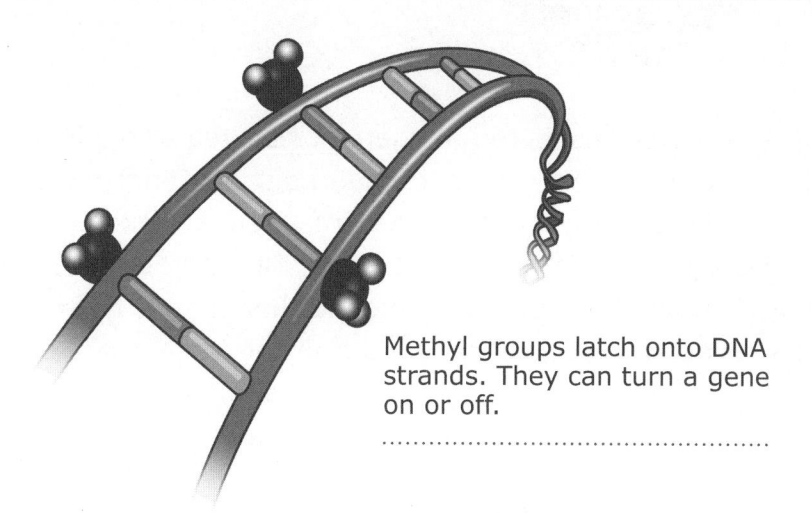

Notes

Notes

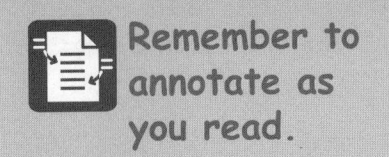

23   As Meaney suspected, epigenetics played a role in this difference. The scientists found distinct differences between methyl patterns in the brain cells of licked babies and those of unlicked babies. The mother's licking flipped switches on the baby's gene that shapes how rats respond to stress—showing that the behavior of one animal can sculpt the epigenetic clay of another animal.

24   But Meaney and his colleagues didn't stop there.

25   The scientists believed they could flip gene switches on fearful rats, causing them to become brave. And in 2007, the scientists discovered they were right. By injecting a chemical into rats, the scientists wiped out the animals' methyl markers and changed rat behavior. Scared rats became brave.

26   The ability to chemically flip methyl switches can help treat human diseases. For instance, doctors can cure specific forms of leukemia (cancer of the blood or bone marrow) by using chemicals to flip methyl switches. Other scientists, including Randy Jirtle, are exploring the role of epigenetics in diseases like schizophrenia (an illness marked by deterioration of the thought processes), depression (an illness characterized by a feeling of such sadness that the sufferer can't live a normal life) and autism (an illness that makes it difficult to communicate with other people).

27   Jirtle explains, "I want to find the genes in humans that are involved in brain development, which, as a consequence, are involved in just about every neurological disorder we have." And once Jirtle finds the genes, he'll look for the methyl groups that affect them. He believes he may find cures this way.

28   So why are gene switches so flippable? Maybe the answer lies in common sense rather than in lab studies. Think of this: Environments change constantly—forests change to grasslands, and grasslands change to deserts. Environments within and around our cells change, thanks to parasites and viruses. Social environments change too: A nurturing environment can become hostile with a stroke of bad luck. No matter how we look at it, humans and other organisms live in constantly changing environments.

Humans and other organisms must adapt to constantly changing environments. Here a prairie is becoming a desert.

29   On the other hand, an organism's genome—or set of genetic instructions—doesn't change quickly. For example, humans now look a lot like humans from 200,000 years ago, even though parents pass on a jumbled mixture of genes to their offspring. How does something as steady as a genome cope with something as changeable as the environment? Perhaps epigenetics is the answer.

30   Moshe Szyf at McGill University says that epigenetics may offer a way to help our unchanging genes cope with sudden changes in their, or our, environment.

31   Changing what's on our genes appears to be easier than changing what's in them. And that may help explain how life so readily adapts to our ever-changing environment.

Notes

What's On Your Genes? | Unit 2 • Genes & Heredity

Close Reading and Collaborative Conversations

What Does the Text Say?	How Does the Text Work?
1. What are methyl groups? Explain what they are in relation to genes.	1. What purpose does the author have in introducing the research of Gregor Mendel in paragraph 4?
2. What causes epigenetic changes? List at least three causes from this article.	2. This article is from a publication called *Student Science*. What information in the text implies that the author intended this to be read by younger people?
3. According to paragraphs 28 through 31, what might be the evolutionary purpose of epigenetic changes?	3. In paragraph 27, find the word "neurological." Based on context clues, what does that word mean?

Unit 2 • Genes & Heredity   What's On Your Genes?

What Does the Text Mean?

1. How does the information in "What's On Your Genes?" conflict with the information provided in "Mendel's Discovery"? Why does each article give different information about the inheritance of traits?

2. Identical twins have the same DNA patterns and the same parents (i.e. their parents' diet is not an issue). How might epigenetic changes described in this article make the identical twins end up looking or acting different?

3. The author describes several experiments on animals and also describes how the results have led to discoveries about how to better care for sick humans. Do you think this article makes a good case for the value of performing painful tests on animals? Explain your reasoning using evidence from the article.

What's On Your Genes? Unit 2 • Genes & Heredity

Write About the Text

Argument Writing Prompt

After reading "What's On Your Genes?" write an essay answering the question: Are experiments on animals important for the understanding of genetic science? Support your opinion with evidence from the text.

Plan your response using this graphic organizer. Use your annotations and your notes on pages 46–53 to find evidence for your essay.

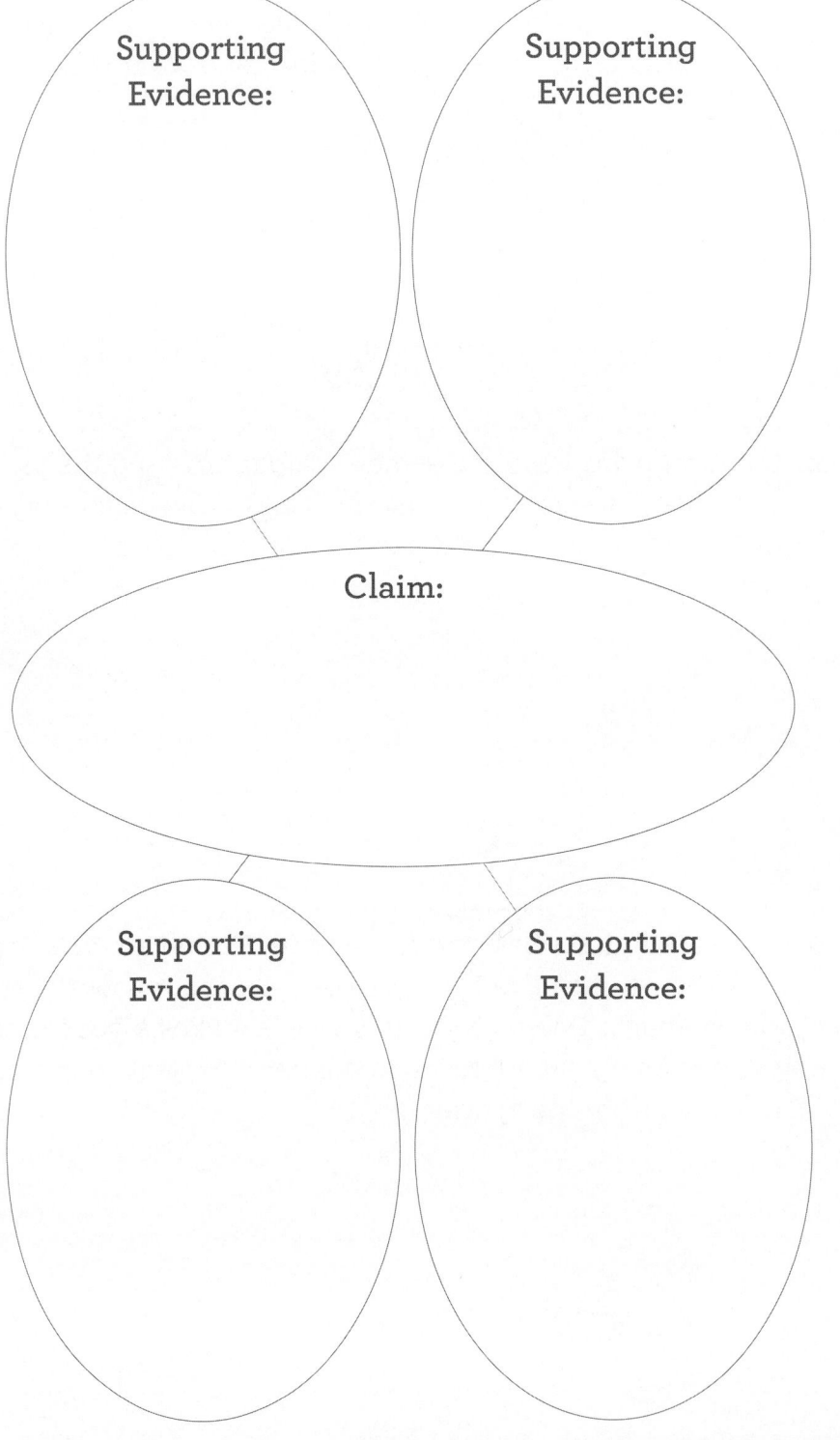

- Supporting Evidence:
- Supporting Evidence:
- Claim:
- Supporting Evidence:
- Supporting Evidence:

Writer's Checklist

- ❏ I introduced the topic and stated my claim.
- ❏ I acknowledged opposing claims.
- ❏ I supported my claim with evidence and logical reasoning.
- ❏ I used transitions to make connections and clarify ideas.
- ❏ I used a formal style.
- ❏ I included a concluding statement.

Wrap Up
Check Your Understanding

1. Pick three statements below that are accurate explanations of methyl groups.

   ☐ They change the genetic code in an organism's DNA.

   ☐ They control whether or not genetic information is expressed.

   ☐ They carry the information that controls fur color in mice.

   ☐ They are affected by food that our parents eat before we are born.

   ☐ They can be switched on or off using chemicals.

   ☐ They have been proven to control the expression of depression and schizophrenia.

   ☐ They are more difficult to change than genetic information.

2. This question has two parts. Answer Part A first. Then answer Part B.

   Part A Why is Randy Jirtle quoted many times in this article?

   A. He is a noted expert on the history of genetic research.

   B. He discovered that epigenetic changes in fetuses could be controlled by the diet of their mothers.

   C. He discovered that epigenetic changes could be inherited.

   D. He discovered that the diet of fathers might affect babies.

   Part B What evidence from the text best supports your answer?

   A. "... fed pregnant mice a particular diet that turned off the Agouti gene in the mama mice's babies."

   B. "... showed that babies could inherit epigenetic changes—a scenario never before imagined by geneticists."

   C. "However, daughters of fat dads did develop health problems related to obesity."

   D. "The mice have the same DNA in the same order on the same chromosomes."

Wrap Up
Check Your Understanding

3. In paragraph 23, the author uses the phrase <u>sculpt the epigenetic clay</u> to explain how behavior of one individual towards another can affect methyl switches. What is an accurate definition of that phrase as its used in the article?

   A. It's a simile, stating that methyl switches on one individual can be affected by the actions of another individual like a sculptor molds clay.

   B. It's a metaphor which implies that methyl switches on one individual can be affected by the actions of another individual like a sculptor molds clay.

   C. It's a hyperbole, which exaggerates the effects of one's individual actions on the methyl switches of another individual.

   D. It's a historical reference to a time when genes were thought of more simply, as clay-like elements.

4. Which statement accurately summarizes the main idea of the article, "What's On Your Genes?"

   A. The discovery of epigenetic changes has made the research of actual genetic inheritance irrelevant.

   B. The discovery of epigenetics overshadowed more than 100 years of genetics research with information that changed the way genetics is understood.

   C. Scientists who research epigenetics conduct many painful experiments on rats and mice.

   D. Epigenetic changes are a new frontier of genetic research, and scientists are continuing to discover ways that these changes affect health and behavior.

Unit 2 • Genes & Heredity Read and Write Across Texts

Read and Write Across Texts

Plan your essay using this graphic organizer.
Use your annotations and the notes you've taken on each passage to identify supporting evidence for your essay.

Introduction:

Evidence from "Mendel's Discovery":

Informative/Explanatory Writing Prompt

After reading the three passages, write an essay answering the question: How has understanding of the way traits are passed from one generation to the next changed over time? Support your position with examples from the texts.

Writer's Checklist

❏ I introduced the topic clearly.
❏ I used evidence and facts to develop the topic.
❏ I clarified relationships between ideas with transitions
❏ I used precise language and vocabulary.
❏ I used a formal style.
❏ I included a concluding statement.

Read and Write Across Texts

Unit 2 • Genes & Heredity

Evidence from "Fancy Feather Gene":

Evidence from "What's On Your Genes?":

Conclusion:

Unit 3
The Constitution

Table of Contents

Letters from the Convention. 60

The Constitutional Convention Begins 66

Benjamin Franklin's Speech
at the Constitutional Convention. 76

Letters from the Convention

In May of 1787, 55 state delegates began to gather in Philadelphia for the Constitutional Convention. The delegates wrote letters to friends and family describing their initial thoughts and experiences during the convention. These are excerpts from a few letters.

1. To William Short, secretary to Thomas Jefferson
2. From James Madison, a delegate from Virginia and the author of the Virginia Plan, which was a model for the Constitution.

3. June 6, 1787

4. The Convention has been formed about 12 days. It contains in several instances the most respectable characters in the U.S. and in general may be said to be the best contribution of talents the States could make for the occasion. What the result of the experiment may be is among the arcana[1] of futurity. Our affairs are considered on all hands as at a most serious crisis. No hope is entertained from the existing Confederacy. And the eyes and hopes of all are turned towards this new assembly. The result therefore whatever it may be must have a material influence on our destiny, and, on that of the cause of republican liberty. The personal characters of the members promise much. The spirit which they bring with them seems in general equally promising. But the labor is great indeed; whether we consider the real or imaginary difficulties within doors or without doors.

---

[1] arcana: mysterious information

Unit 3 • The Constitution   Letters from the Convention

5   To Thomas Jefferson, who was serving as American Minister to France during the Constitutional Convention.

6   From George Washington, a delegate from Virginia. He was voted the President of the Convention on May 25, 1787

7   May 30, 1787

8   The business of this convention is yet too much in embryo to form any opinion of the result. Much is expected from it by some, but little by others, and nothing by a few. That something is necessary, all will agree; from the situation of the General Government (if it can be called a government) is shaken to its foundation and liable to be overset by every blast. In a word, it is at an end, and unless a remedy is soon applied, anarchy and confusion will inevitably ensue.

9   To George Mason Jr., son of the Virginia delegate

10 From George Mason, delegate from Virginia

11 June 01, 1787

12 The eyes of the United States are turned upon this assembly, and their expectations raised to a very anxious degree. May God grant, we may be able to gratify them, by establishing a wise and just government. For my own part, I never before felt myself in such a situation... I would not, upon pecuniary[2] motives, serve in this convention for a thousand pounds per day. The revolt from Great Britain and the formations of our new governments at that time, were nothing compared to the great business now before us...

13 All communications of the proceedings are forbidden during the sitting of the Convention; this I think was a necessary precaution to prevent misrepresentations or mistakes; there being a material difference between the appearance of a subject in its first crude and undigested shape, and after it shall have been properly matured and arranged.

[2] pecuniary: financial

Letters from the Convention — Unit 3 • The Constitution

Close Reading and Collaborative Conversations

What Does the Text Say?	How Does the Text Work?
1. What are the big ideas in these letters? Turn to a partner and summarize what you have read.	**1.** In Washington's letter, why is the term "embryo" an apt metaphor for the Constitutional Convention as Washington describes it?
2. Why does Mason say communications of the proceedings are forbidden? Paraphrase what he wrote.	**2.** Is Mason hopeful about the convention? Use details from his letter to support your answer.
3. What positive aspects of the convention does Madison's letter emphasize?	**3.** What might Madison mean about "real or imaginary difficulties within doors or without doors"? What do "within" and "without" refer to?

What Does the Text Mean?

1. In his letter, what does Washington write about his thoughts on the fate of the government? Is he hopeful or doubtful? Which details from his letter support this idea?

2. How were Mason and Washington's roles different? How might their roles relate to their attitudes toward the convention?

3. After reviewing the letters, explain whether the three writers disagree on any facts, or if they only have different interpretations of the convention.

Write About the Text

Informative/Explanatory Writing Prompt

After reading "Letters from the Convention," write an essay explaining the main purpose of the Constitutional Convention. What problem was it set up to solve? What did these men think of the effort being made to solve the problem? Support your discussion with evidence from the text.

Plan your response using this graphic organizer. Use your annotations and your notes on pages 60–63 to find text evidence.

Introduction:

Example:

Supporting Text Evidence:

Example:

Supporting Text Evidence:

Conclusion:

Writer's Checklist

- ❏ I introduced the topic clearly.
- ❏ I used evidence and facts to develop the topic.
- ❏ I clarified relationships between ideas with transitions.
- ❏ I used precise language and vocabulary.
- ❏ I used a formal style.
- ❏ I have a concluding statement.

Wrap Up
Check Your Understanding

1. This question has two parts. Answer Part A first. Then answer Part B.

   Part A When Washington writes that the General Government is "liable to be overset by every blast," what does he mean?

   A. There is a danger of both actual violence and also disorganization.

   B. There is only danger of actual violence, but not disorganization.

   C. There is only danger of disorganization, but not actual violence.

   D. There is no actual danger of anything bad happening.

   Part B What evidence in the text supports the answer you chose?

   A. "shaken to its foundation"

   B. "a remedy is soon applied"

   C. "anarchy and confusion"

   D. "inevitably ensue"

2. What point does Washington believe everyone agrees on?

   A. Some kind of governmental change is necessary.

   B. The return of the British government is necessary.

   C. The Convention will solve America's problems.

   D. The country is headed for anarchy and confusion.

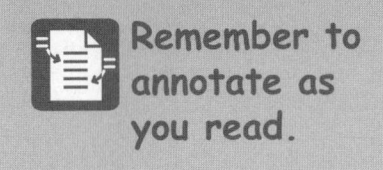

The Constitutional Convention Begins

by Roger Bruns

May 25, 1787

Freshly spread dirt covered the cobblestone street in front of the Pennsylvania State House, protecting the men inside from the sound of passing carriages and carts. Guards stood at the entrances to ensure that the curious were kept at a distance. Robert Morris of Pennsylvania opened the proceedings with a nomination—Gen. George Washington for the presidency of the Constitutional Convention. The vote was unanimous. With characteristic ceremonial modesty, the general expressed his embarrassment at his lack of qualifications to preside over such an august body and apologized for any errors into which he might fall in the course of its deliberations.

To many of those assembled, especially to the small, boyish-looking, 36-year-old delegate from Virginia, James Madison, the general's mere presence boded well for the convention. The illustrious Washington gave to the gathering an air of importance and legitimacy. But his decision to attend the convention had been an agonizing one. The Father of the Country had almost remained at home.

4   Washington was suffering from rheumatism, despondent over the loss of a brother, and absorbed in the management of Mount Vernon. He also doubted that the convention would accomplish very much or that many men of stature would attend. Because his doubts, Washington delayed accepting the invitation to attend for several months. Torn between the hazards of lending his reputation to a gathering perhaps doomed to failure and the chance that the public would view his reluctance to attend with a critical eye, the general finally agreed to make the trip. James Madison was pleased.

The Articles of Confederation

5   The determined Madison had for several years insatiably studied history and political theory searching for a solution to the political and economic dilemmas he saw plaguing America. The Virginian's labors convinced him of the futility and weakness of confederacies of independent states. America's own government under the Articles of Confederation, Madison was convinced, had to be replaced. In force since 1781, the articles seemed to Madison woefully inadequate. With the states retaining considerable power, the central government, he believed, had insufficient power to regulate commerce. It could not tax and was generally impotent in setting commercial policy. It could not effectively support a war effort. It had little power to settle quarrels between states. Saddled with this weak government, the states were on the brink of economic disaster. The evidence was overwhelming. Congress was attempting to function with a depleted treasury. Paper money was flooding the country, creating extraordinary inflation—a pound of tea in some areas could be purchased for a tidy $100. And the depressed condition of business was taking its toll on many small farmers. Some of them were being thrown in jail for debt. Numerous farms were being confiscated and sold for taxes.

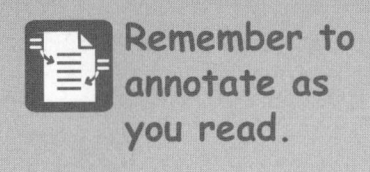

6   In 1786 some of the farmers had fought back. Led by Daniel Shays, a group of armed men prevented the circuit court from sitting at Northampton, MA, and threatened to seize muskets stored in the arsenal at Springfield. Although the insurrection was put down by state troops, the incident confirmed the fears of many wealthy men that anarchy was just around the corner. Embellished day after day in the press, the uprising made upper-class Americans shudder as they imagined hordes of vicious outlaws descending upon innocent citizens. Washington wrote to Madison: "Wisdom and good examples are necessary at this time to rescue the political machine from the impending storm."

7   Madison thought he had the answer. He wanted a strong central government to provide order and stability. "Let it be tried then," he wrote, "whether any middle ground can be taken which will at once support a due supremacy of the national authority," while maintaining state power only when "subordinately useful." The resolute Virginian looked to the Constitutional Convention to forge a new government in this mold.

Notes

8   The convention had its specific origins in a proposal offered by Madison and John Tyler in the Virginia assembly. They proposed that the Continental Congress be given power to regulate commerce throughout the Confederation. Through their efforts in the assembly a plan was devised inviting the several states to attend a convention at Annapolis, MD, in September 1786 to discuss commercial problems. Madison and a young lawyer from New York named Alexander Hamilton issued a report on the meeting in Annapolis. They called upon Congress to summon delegates of all of the states to meet for the purpose of revising the Articles of Confederation. Although the report was widely viewed as a usurpation of congressional authority, the Congress did issue a formal call to the states for a convention. To Madison it represented the supreme chance to reverse the country's trend. And as the delegations gathered in Philadelphia, its importance was not lost to others. George Mason, wrote to his son, "The Eyes of the United States are turned upon this Assembly and their Expectations raised to a very anxious Degree. May God Grant that we may be able to gratify them, by establishing a wise and just Government."

9   Seventy-four delegates were appointed to the convention, of which 55 actually attended sessions. Rhode Island was the only state that refused to send delegates. Dominated by men wedded to paper currency, low taxes, and popular government, Rhode Island's leaders refused to participate in what they saw as a conspiracy to overthrow the established government. Other Americans also had their suspicions. Patrick Henry refused to attend, declaring he "smelt a rat." He suspected, correctly, that Madison had in mind the creation of a powerful central government and the subversion of the authority of the state legislatures. Henry along with many other political leaders, believed that the state governments offered the chief protection for personal liberties. He was determined not to lend a hand to any proceeding that seemed to pose a threat to that protection.

The Constitutional Convention lasted through the summer. The first draft of the Constitution was accepted on August 6, 1787. On September 17, 38 of the 41 delegates signed the constitution.

an excerpt from Introduction by Roger A. Bruns to *A More Perfect Union: The Creation of the U.S. Constitution.*

Close Reading and Collaborative Conversations

What Does the Text Say?	How Does the Text Work?
1. What is this passage mostly about? Turn to a partner and summarize the passage.	1. How do the details about the setting of the convention and Washington's emotional and physical state in the first section help set the tone for this text?
2. What was Madison's role in the convention? Use details from the passage to support your answer.	2. How does paragraph 6 develop and refine the idea that the nation was in crisis?
3. What problems were the Constitutional Convention tasked with solving?	3. Is the author of this piece sympathetic to Patrick Henry's viewpoint, as stated in the last paragraph? Explain your reasoning using evidence from the text.

What Does the Text Mean?

1. What conclusions can you draw about Madison after reading both his letter in the previous selection, and the description of him and his goals in this selection?

2. Why did it bode well for the Constitutional Convention to have Washington as its president? What other details from the text support your response?

3. Why does the author present viewpoints of those opposed to the Constitutional Convention, such as that of Patrick Henry or the leaders of the state of Rhode Island?

The Constitutional Convention Begins   Unit 3 • The Constitution

Write About the Text

Argument Writing Prompt

After reading "The Constitutional Convention Begins," write an essay answering the question: Was the Constitutional Convention necessary to protect the future of the United States? Support your opinion with evidence from the text.

Plan your response using this graphic organizer. Use your annotations and your notes on pages 66–73 to find evidence for your essay.

Supporting Evidence:

Supporting Evidence:

Claim:

Supporting Evidence:

Supporting Evidence:

Writer's Checklist

- ❏ I introduced a claim.
- ❏ I acknowledged opposing claims.
- ❏ I supported my claim with evidence and logical reasoning.
- ❏ I used words and phrases to make connections and clarify ideas.
- ❏ I used a formal style.
- ❏ I included a concluding statement.

Wrap Up
Check Your Understanding

1. This question has two parts. Answer Part A first. Then answer Part B.

   Part A. In paragraph 2, what does the phrase such an august body mean?

   A. hot and humid person

   B. respected and impressive group

   C. simpleminded and easy-to-lead

   D. curious and open-minded visitors

   Part B. What evidence in the text supports the answer you chose?

   A. "The vote was unanimous."

   B. ". . . the curious were kept at a distance."

   C. "modesty" and "lack of qualifications"

   D. "the course of its deliberations"

2. Which is *not* an example of a weakness of the federal government before the Constitutional Convention?

   A. could not tax

   B. could not form a congress

   C. could not set commercial policy

   D. could not settle quarrels between the states

Passage 3 — Unit 3 • The Constitution

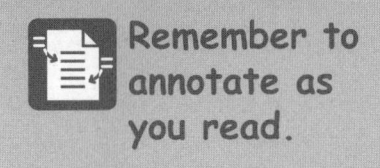

Benjamin Franklin's Speech AT THE CONSTITUTIONAL CONVENTION

On September 15, 1787, the delegates at the Constitutional Convention approved the final version of the Constitution. The states would begin to hold conventions to ratify the new constitution. Before returning home, the delegates met for the last time on September 17. Benjamin Franklin prepared this speech. Because of Franklin's poor health, it was delivered by James Wilson.

1   Mr. President:

2   I confess that I do not entirely approve of this constitution at present. But I am not sure I shall never approve it. For having lived long, I have experienced many instances of being obliged, by better information or fuller consideration, to change opinions even on important subjects, which I once thought right, but found to be otherwise....The older I grow the more apt I am to doubt my own judgment, and to pay more respect to the judgment of others. Most men... think themselves in possession of all truth, and that wherever others differ from them it is so far error. ... Few express it so naturally as a certain French lady. ... In a dispute with her sister, said, I don't know how it happens, but I meet with no body but myself that's always in the right.

3   In these sentiments, Sir, I agree to this Constitution, with all its faults, if they are such. Because I think a general government necessary for us . . .

4   I doubt too whether any other convention we can obtain, may be able to make a better Constitution: For when you assemble a number of men to have the advantage of their joint wisdom, you inevitably assemble with those men all their prejudices, their passions, their errors of opinion, their local interests, and their selfish views. From such an assembly can a perfect production be expected? It therefore astonishes me, Sir, to find this system approaching so near to perfection as it does. And I think it will astonish our enemies, who are waiting with confidence to hear that our councils are confounded… and that our states are on the point of separation…. Thus I consent, Sir, to this constitution because I expect no better, and because I am not sure that it is not the best.

5   The opinions I have had of its errors, I sacrifice to the public good. I have never whispered a syllable of them abroad. Within these walls they were born, and here they shall die. If every one of us in returning to our constituents were to report [his] objections to it…we might prevent its being generally received. Much of the strength and efficiency of any government…depends on the general opinion of the goodness of that government, as well as of the wisdom and integrity of its governors. I hope therefore that for our own sakes and for the sake of our posterity, we shall act heartily and unanimously in recommending this constitution, wherever our influence may extend.

6   On the whole, sir, I cannot help expressing a wish, that every member of the convention, who may still have objections to it, would with me on this occasion doubt a little of his own infallibility, and to make manifest our unanimity, put his name to this instrument.

Benjamin Franklin's Speech   Unit 3 • The Constitution

🗨️ Close Reading and Collaborative Conversations

What Does the Text Say?	How Does the Text Work?
1. What is Benjamin Franklin's speech mostly about? Turn to a partner and summarize the speech.	**1.** In paragraph 2, Franklin makes a joke about "a certain French lady." What is his purpose in making this joke?
2. Does Franklin think a perfect constitution is possible? Explain his reasoning.	**2.** Why does Franklin make a point of mentioning "our enemies"? How does he acknowledge and respond to their viewpoint?
3. Why does Franklin counsel members of the convention against sharing their doubts about the constitution?	**3.** Why do you think Franklin doesn't lay out his specific objections? Use details from his speech to support your answer.

What Does the Text Mean?

1. Franklin's speech is written in a very different tone than the letters presented in the first reading. Explain how and why the tone is different.

2. What is Franklin's overall goal with his speech? How does he hope to influence the delegates? What details from the text support your response?

3. Would James Madison, as described in his own letter in the first reading, and in the text of the second reading, have appreciated Franklin's speech? Why or why not?

Benjamin Franklin's Speech   Unit 3 • The Constitution

Write About the Text

Argument Writing Prompt

After reading "Benjamin Franklin's Speech at the Constitutional Convention," write an essay answering the question: Does Franklin approve of the Constitution or does he disapprove of it? Support your opinion with evidence from the text.

Plan your response using this graphic organizer. Use your annotations and your notes on pages 76–79 to find evidence for your essay.

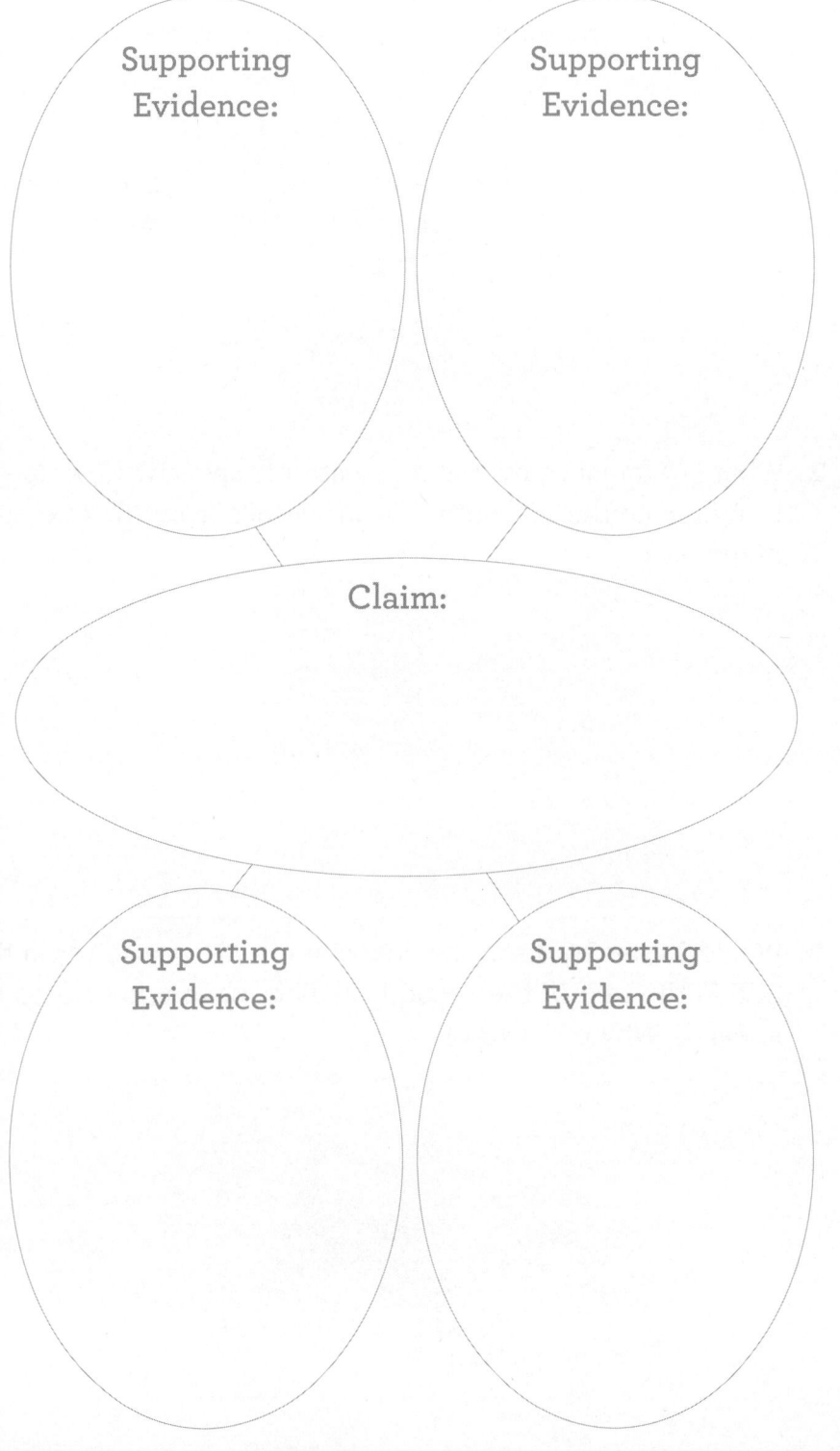

- Supporting Evidence:
- Supporting Evidence:
- Claim:
- Supporting Evidence:
- Supporting Evidence:

Writer's Checklist

❑ I introduced a claim.

❑ I acknowledged opposing claims.

❑ I supported my claim with evidence and logical reasoning.

❑ I used transitions to make connections and clarify ideas.

❑ I used a formal style.

❑ I have a concluding statement.

Wrap Up
Check Your Understanding

1. Pick two arguments that Franklin makes for supporting the Constitution.

    ☐ It is a flawless document that was created by the best men in the country.

    ☐ It will astonish the enemies of the United States.

    ☐ Its mistakes can be fixed when they write the next draft.

    ☐ A general government is necessary for the American people.

    ☐ It's better than the previous Articles of Confederation.

2. This question has two parts. Answer Part A first. Then answer Part B.

    Part A In the last paragraph, what does the word infallibility mean?

    A. doubtfulness

    B. certainty

    C. attitude of objection

    D. wishful

    Part B What evidence from the text best supports your answer?

    A. "may still have objections" and "doubt"

    B. "expressing a wish" and "make manifest"

    C. "on the whole" and "instrument"

    D. "wisdom and integrity" and "heartily and unanimously"

Wrap Up
Check Your Understanding

3. This question has two parts. Answer Part A first. Then answer Part B.

Part A What statement about age might Benjamin Franklin agree with?

- **A.** Aging has made him more certain of his opinions.
- **B.** Aging has allowed him to become more open-minded.
- **C.** Aging has given him a better sense of humor.
- **D.** Aging has made him more confused about things.

Part B What evidence from the text best supports your answer?

- **A.** "I hope therefore that for our own sakes and for the sake of our posterity, we shall act heartily…"
- **B.** "Thus I consent, Sir, to this constitution because I expect no better, and because I am not sure that it is not the best."
- **C.** "The older I grow the more apt I am to doubt my own judgment…"
- **D.** "For having lived long, I have experienced many instances of being obliged, by better information or fuller consideration, to change opinions even on important subjects, which I once thought right, but found to be otherwise."

Unit 3 • The Constitution   Read and Write Across Texts

Read and Write Across Texts

Plan your essay using this graphic organizer. Use your annotations and the notes you've taken on each passage to identify supporting evidence for your essay.

Introduction:

Evidence from "Letters from the Convention":

Informative/Explanatory Writing Prompt

After reading all three passages, write an essay answering the question: What were the challenges that delegates and leaders faced during the Constitutional Convention? Support your position with examples from the texts.

Writer's Checklist

- ❏ I introduced the topic clearly.
- ❏ I used evidence and facts to develop the topic.
- ❏ I clarified relationships between ideas with transitions.
- ❏ I used precise language and vocabulary.
- ❏ I used a formal style.
- ❏ I have a concluding statement.

© Benchmark Education Company, LLC • Grade 8 • Accessing Complex Texts Now!

Read and Write Across Texts

Unit 3 • The Constitution

Evidence from "The Constitutional Convention Begins":

Evidence from "Benjamin Franklin's Speech at the Constitutional Convention":

Conclusion:

Unit 4
Transformation

Table of Contents
The Myth of Pygmalion. 86
Operation Sherry. 92
Pygmalion 100

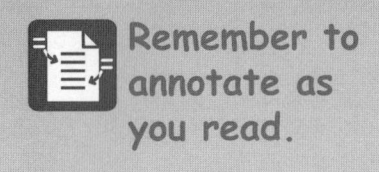

THE MYTH OF PYGMALION

1. I am Pygmalion, the king of Cyprus with the reputation for detesting woman. Perhaps these strong feelings emerged in me after being rejected by dozens of fair maidens; I took them for expensive meals followed by dancing in the Metropolis, but they all wanted nothing more to do with me. It is a mystery to me why these women did not fall head over heels in love with me. I had the looks, money, personality, and charisma, and I could be very romantic. (I love walks in the moonlight and rainy Saturdays.)

2. Most women, like my mother, are rude and selfish creatures who require all too much attention and praise. Or, so I thought. So I decided to live out my days as a bachelor.

3. I am a gifted sculptor who works with ivory and one day my hands started on a project that resulted in a form so perfect and lovely. Her skin was smooth and polished, her eyes were as sparkling as diamonds, and her face was gentle and kind, yet stunning. I was speechless at the figure before me, at what I had created. It was a woman I called Galatea.

4. I could not take my eyes off her, and all I wanted was to be close to her and to adorn her. I placed rings on her fingers and a strand of pearls hung about her neck. Sometimes I pretended, just as a child might, that she was real, and I would talk to her and tell her all my deep, dark secrets. I believed that she was listening and cared deeply for me.

5. I presented my love with tokens of affection, such as polished stones, little birds, pieces of amber, and flowers of all sorts. All I wanted was for her to become more, to be real; I wanted her to be human and alive, and my wife.

Unit 4 • Transformation

The Myth of Pygmalion

6   It was at the great Festival of Venus that I stood before the altar and quietly whispered to the gods, "Ye gods, who can do all things, give me, I pray you, a wife." I dared not say "my ivory sculpture," but I did say, "one like my ivory sculpture."

7   Just then, the goddess Venus heard my plea and the flame on the altar shot up three times in a fiery point into the air.

8   When I returned home to Galatea, I touched her face. To my great astonishment, something had changed within her; she was warm to the touch. My creation was turning into a living, breathing woman.

9   All at once, her eyes were fixed on me and she smiled brightly. She whispered my name and then, I embraced my true love.

10 At our nuptials, we gave thanks to the goddess Venus, who made my dreams come true. With Galatea at my side, I was a changed man because she taught me how to love.

Notes

The Myth of Pygmalion　　　　　　　　　　　　　　　　Unit 4 • Transformation

Close Reading and Collaborative Conversations

What Does the Text Say?	How Does the Text Work?
1. What is this passage mostly about? Turn to a partner and summarize "The Myth of Pygmalion."	1. How does the author let the reader know that the statue will turn into a woman and that he will marry her?
2. How does Pygmalion feel about real women? What does he do because of those feelings?	2. What does Pygmalion do that shows his love for the statue?
3. When Pygmalion leaves the festival, does he know that the statue will be turned into a woman? Explain your answer.	3. Reread paragraph 4. What does "adorn" mean? What context clues help you to know the meaning?

Unit 4 • Transformation

The Myth of Pygmalion

What Does the Text Mean?

1. Reread paragraphs 1–4. What does Pygmalion get from the statue that he does not get from real women?

2. Pygmalion is a grown man, a king, but he displays childlike characteristics. What details from the text support this inference?

3. How does Pygmalion change during the passage? Use evidence from the text to support your response.

Write About the Text

Informative/Explanatory Writing Prompt

After Reading "The Myth of Pygmalion," write a paragraph in which you describe Pygmalion's relationship with the statue and how that relationship came about. Support your discussion with evidence from the text.

Writer's Checklist

- ❏ I introduced the topic.
- ❏ I developed the topic with facts, details, and evidence.
- ❏ I used transitions to connect ideas.
- ❏ I used precise language.
- ❏ I used a formal style.
- ❏ I included a concluding statement.

Plan your response using this graphic organizer. Use your annotations and your notes on pages 86–89 to find text evidence.

Key Idea/Event:

Details:
-
-
-

Key Idea/Event:

Details:
-
-
-

Topic Sentence:

Key Idea/Event:

Details:
-
-
-

Conclusion:

Wrap Up
Check Your Understanding

1. This question has two parts. Read this sentence from paragraph 10 in the passage. Then, answer the questions. Answer Part A first, then answer Part B.

   > At our nuptials, we gave thanks to the goddess Venus, who made my dreams come true.

   Part A What is the meaning of nuptials as used in this sentence?
   - A. birth
   - B. home
   - C. wedding
   - D. life

   Part B Which phrase from the passage helps you understand the meaning of nuptials?
   - A. "made my dreams come true"
   - B. "she taught me how to love"
   - C. "her eyes were fixed on me and she smiled brightly"
   - D. "My creation was turning into a living, breathing woman."

2. Decide which statements belong in a summary of the passage and number them in the correct order.
   - ___ Pygmalion sculpts a statue.
   - ___ The statue falls in love with Pygmalion.
   - ___ Pygmalion carefully wraps the statue so nothing will happen to it.
   - ___ Pygmalion falls in love with his own creation.
   - ___ Pygmalion falls in love with a woman at the festival.
   - ___ Venus thinks the statue made by Pygmalion is beautiful.
   - ___ Pygmalion and the former statue, now a woman, get married.

Passage 2

Unit 4 • Transformation

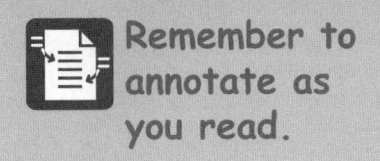

OPERATION SHERRY

1. At the box office, my knees are shaking, but somehow I muster the courage to ask for my ticket. In the last moment, I am able to do what Brooke told me to do when she said that I need to believe in The Transformation. I tell myself that I am Sherry, a seventeen-year-old movie-going hipster.

2. It doesn't matter so much that the "friends" I am standing with are not my friends at all, just a group of high school girls that happen to know Brooke's older sister. They have granted me permission to stand with them. The important thing is that Operation Sherry is a success because I am in! And I'm about to see "From Here to There" starring the irresistible Nick Heartstone!

3. It really doesn't matter that my ankles are bleeding. And I don't mind that my toes are being squished in ways they never were before (though I vow never to wear heels again). What matters is that I have completed The Transformation from thirteen-year-old girl into seventeen-year-old woman in just a few short hours.

4. Brooke was the mastermind behind Operation Sherry. After listening to me complaining about not being allowed to go to the movie, she had an idea. Brooke convinced me that with the right clothes, perfect hair and makeup, plus a little confidence, I could easily pass for seventeen. I was hesitant at first but Brooke, who loves television makeovers and dreams of working in fashion, can be very persuasive.

Unit 4 • Transformation

Operation Sherry

5   Brooke did a superb job dressing me. I abandoned my usual T-shirt and jeans and she outfitted me in clothes borrowed from her older sister's closet. Then she did my hair and spent what felt like hours—though it was more like fifteen minutes—doing my makeup. She slathered a pound of foundation on my face, and then came the eye shadow, mascara, eyeliner, and lipstick. I had a hard time keeping my eyes open—to Brooke's annoyance.

6   The Transformation was complete once I was able to do a couple laps around Brooke's house without tripping in the heels. Brooke offered encouraging words that convinced me the plan would work. Operation Sherry was a go!

7   I didn't want to have to sneak or lie, but I just had to see this movie, and I just knew my dad wouldn't take me. There's no way that my dad, who happens to be a detective at the third precinct, would go for his thirteen-year-old daughter at an R-rated movie. He left me no choice.

8   The high school girls that so graciously walked into the movie with me go one way and I go the other. With a few minutes to spare before the 2:00 showing, I decide to stop by the refreshment stand for a tub of popcorn. As I wait, I text Brooke letting her know prematurely that Operation Sherry is a success! Brooke texts back a smiley face.

9   I notice some commotion at the other end of the refreshment stand. I can hear the two men shouting at each other.

10   "Hey! What are you doing? I was here first." The bigger guy is hovering over the smaller guy, poking his finger into the man's chest.

Notes

Passage 2 *continued* — Unit 4 • Transformation

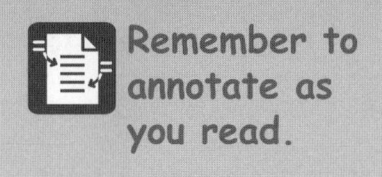

11 "If you touch me again, man, I'm gonna. . . ."

12 "Please, I'm going to have to ask you both to calm down," the girl working behind pleads, her voice sounding a little shaky.

13 The men ignore her pleas and keeping arguing. The scene is entertaining; a little pre-theater theater. Then I see two police officers walk through the front doors and head to the refreshment counter.

14 I figure the show is over and I make my way toward my feature presentation. I am just thinking how I should look like this more often, that for the first time ever people are taking me seriously, and I feel so grown up. The Transformation of Sherry was long overdue. But then, I feel a poking on my shoulder.

15 "Huh, what's up?" I ask, and turn around.

16 "I thought that was you. Sherry? Are you wearing makeup?" asks Dad, smiling.

17 Could anything be worse? Seconds away from the movie and all of a sudden, I run into Dad. He was called to control the argument at the refreshment stand. Really?

18 Dad is looking at me like I have two heads. But he isn't angry because he doesn't know that I am trying to sneak into a movie that I am not supposed to see. He is just a little puzzled by the way that I am dressed. But Dad is smiling at me, and the whole charade is just too much for me, so I spill the beans, and tell Dad everything. And you know what he says? If I can wait until the next showing, he will take me to the movie and out for pizza. Is he great or what? So I hug him and accidentally smear lipstick all over his face.

19   In the bathroom, I catch myself in the mirror and realize how silly I have been, rushing to grow up. The Transformation is quickly washed away with soap, water, and a bunch of paper towels. When I look like my thirteen-year-old self again, Dad says, "There's my girl." He hugs me and asks if I'm sure I want to see "From Here to There." Strangest thing happens; I say I have changed my mind, and we end up at a sweet and sappy G-rated movie. And it is awesome!

Notes

Operation Sherry | **Unit 4 • Transformation**

Close Reading and Collaborative Conversations

What Does the Text Say?	How Does the Text Work?
1. What is the big idea of this passage? Turn to a partner and summarize "Operation Sherry."	1. How would you describe the tone in this story?
2. Whose idea was it for Sherry to sneak into the movie?	2. Reread paragraphs 4–5. How does the reader know that Sherry does not usually wear makeup or style her hair?
3. How does Sherry run into her father at the movies?	3. What does the following sentence tell the reader? "Dad is looking at me like I have two heads."

Unit 4 • Transformation   Operation Sherry

What Does the Text Mean?

1. Reread paragraph 1. How is Sherry feeling at this point? Use evidence from the text to support your response.

2. How do Sherry's feelings about The Transformation change throughout "Operation Sherry"?

3. How would you describe Sherry? Choose a couple of character traits shown in the passage and explain why you chose them.

Operation Sherry · Unit 4 • Transformation

Write About the Text

Argument Writing Prompt

After reading "Operation Sherry," write a paragraph in which you discuss Sherry's actions in the story and evaluate what these actions say about her. Support your position with evidence from the text.

Plan your response using this graphic organizer. Use your annotations and your notes on pages 92–97 to find text evidence.

Introduction:

Example:

Supporting Text Evidence:

Example:

Supporting Text Evidence:

Conclusion:

Writer's Checklist

- ❏ I introduced the topic and clearly stated my claim.
- ❏ I acknowledged opposing claims.
- ❏ I supported my claim with evidence and logical reasoning.
- ❏ I used transitions to clarify connections between ideas.
- ❏ I used a formal style.
- ❏ I have a concluding statement.

Unit 4 • Transformation — Operation Sherry

Wrap Up
Check Your Understanding

1. This question has two parts. Answer Part A first, then answer Part B.

    Part A What is the meaning of the word <u>charade</u> in paragraph 18?

    A. pretending

    B. waiting

    C. game

    D. confusion

    Part B Which phrase or sentence from the passage helps you understand the meaning of <u>charade</u>?

    A. "Dad is looking at me like I have two heads."

    B. "But Dad is smiling at me."

    C. "I spill the beans, and tell Dad everything."

    D. "If I can wait until the next showing, he will take me to the movie and out for pizza."

2. Decide which statements belong in a summary of the passage. Number them in order.

    ___ Sherry makes friends with some of the teenagers.

    ___ Sherry often lies in order to do things she wants to do.

    ___ Sherry practices walking on high heels.

    ___ Brooke wants to work in fashion.

    ___ Sherry likes pretending to be older.

    ___ Sherry promises her dad that she won't go to the movie without him.

    ___ Sherry doesn't like the way she looks in the makeup.

PYGMALION

AN EXCERPT FROM ACT 2
by George Bernard Shaw

1. In Act 1 of the play, Henry Higgins is observing Eliza Doolittle and taking notes as she sells flowers on the street. When it begins to rain, Higgins, Eliza, an older gentleman, and several bystanders take shelter under an awning. Higgins impresses everyone with his ability to figure out where someone is from based on their accents. When Higgins explains that he is a scholar of phonetics, the older gentleman introduces himself as Colonel Pickering, another scholar of phonetics. The two men talk and during the conversation, Higgins brags that "within three months I could pass that girl [Eliza] off as a duchess at an ambassador's garden party."

CHARACTERS

Henry Higgins
a scholar of phonetics and dialects

Colonel Pickering
a scholar of phonetics and Indians dialects who is visiting Higgins

Mrs. Pearce
housekeeper

Eliza Doolittle
flower girl

ACT 2

2. (Higgins's laboratory in Wimpole Street. It is a room on the first floor. The double doors are in the middle of the back hall; and persons entering find in the corner to their right two tall file cabinets at right angles to one another against the walls. In this corner stands a flat writing-table, on which are a phonograph, a laryngoscope, several tuning-forks of different sizes, a life-size image of half a human head, showing in section the vocal organs, and a box containing a supply of wax cylinders for the phonograph.)

3   (*Pickering is seated at the table, and Higgins is standing up near him. He appears in the morning light as a robust, vital, appetizing sort of man of forty or thereabouts. He is of the energetic, scientific type, heartily, even violently interested in everything that can be studied as a scientific subject, and careless about himself and other people, including their feelings. He is, in fact, but for his years and size, rather like a very impetuous baby.*)

4   **MRS. PEARCE:** (*hesitating, evidently perplexed*) A young woman wants to see you, sir.

5   **HIGGINS:** A young woman! What does she want?

6   **MRS. PEARCE:** Well, sir, she says you'll be glad to see her when you know what she's come about. She's quite a common girl, sir. Very common indeed. I should have sent her away, only I thought perhaps you wanted her to talk into your machines. I hope I've not done wrong, sir—

7   **HIGGINS:** Oh, that's all right, Mrs. Pearce. Has she an interesting accent?

8   **MRS. PEARCE:** Oh, something dreadful, sir, really. I don't know how you can take an interest in it.

9   **HIGGINS:** (*to Pickering*) Lets have her up. Show her up, Mrs. Pearce.

10 **MRS. PEARCE:** (*only half resigned to it*) Very well, sir. It's for you to say. (*She goes downstairs.*)

11 **HIGGINS:** This is rather a bit of luck. I'll show you how I make records. We'll set her talking and then we'll get her on the phonograph so that you can turn it on as often as you like with the written transcript before you.

12 **MRS. PEARCE:** (*returning*) This is the young woman, sir.

13   (*The flower girl enters in a hat with three ostrich feathers, orange, sky-blue, and red. She has a nearly clean apron, and the shoddy coat has been tidied a little. The pathos of this deplorable figure, with its innocent vanity and consequential air, touches Pickering, who has already straightened himself in the presence of Mrs. Pearce. But as to Higgins, the only distinction he makes between men and women is that when he is neither bullying nor exclaiming to the heavens against some featherweight cross, he coaxes women as a child coaxes its nurse when it wants to get anything out of her.*)

14   **HIGGINS:** (*brusquely, recognizing her with unconcealed disappointment, and at once, babylike, making an intolerable grievance of it*) Why, this is the girl I jotted down last night. She's no use. Be off with you.

15   **THE FLOWER GIRL:** Don't you be so saucy. You ain't heard what I come for yet. (*to Mrs. Pearce, who is waiting at the door for further instruction*) Did you tell him I come in a taxi?

16   **MRS. PEARCE:** Nonsense, girl! What do you think a gentleman like Mr. Higgins cares what you came in?

17   **THE FLOWER GIRL:** Oh, we are proud! He ain't above giving lessons, not him. I heard him say so. Well, I ain't come here to ask for any compliment; and if my money's not good enough I can go elsewhere.

18   **HIGGINS:** Good enough for what?

19   **THE FLOWER GIRL:** Good enough for ye-oo. Now you know, don't you? I'm come to have lessons, I am. And to pay for 'em too: make no mistake.

20   **HIGGINS:** W e l l ! ! ! (*recovering his breath with a gasp*) What do you expect me to say to you?

21   **THE FLOWER GIRL:** Well, if you was a gentleman, you might ask me to sit down, I think. Don't I tell you I'm bringing you business?

22   **HIGGINS:** Pickering, shall we ask this baggage to sit down or shall we throw her out of the window?

23   **THE FLOWER GIRL:** (*running away in terror*) Ah-ah-ah-ow-ow-ow-oo! (*wounded and whimpering*) I won't be called a baggage when I've offered to pay like any lady.

24   (*Motionless, the two men stare at her from the other side of the room, amazed.*)

25   **PICKERING:** (*gently*) What is it you want, my girl?

26   **THE FLOWER GIRL:** I want to be a lady in a flower shop 'stead of selling at the corner of Tottenham Court Road. But they won't take me unless I can talk more genteel. He said he could teach me. Well, here I am ready to pay him—not asking any favor—and he treats me as if I was dirt.

27   **MRS. PEARCE:** How can you be such a foolish ignorant girl as to think you could afford to pay Mr. Higgins?

28   **THE FLOWER GIRL:** Why shouldn't I? I know what lessons cost as well as you do; and I'm ready to pay.

29   **HIGGINS:** How much?

30   **THE FLOWER GIRL:** (*coming back to him, triumphant*) Now you're talking! I thought you'd come off it when you saw a chance of getting back a bit of what you chucked at me last night.

31   **HIGGINS:** Sit down.

32   **THE FLOWER GIRL:** Oh, if you're going to make a compliment of it—

33   **HIGGINS:** (*thundering at her*) Sit down.

34   **MRS. PEARCE:** (*severely*) Sit down, girl. Do as you're told. (*She places the stray chair between Higgins and Pickering, and stands behind it waiting for the girl to sit down.*)

35   **THE FLOWER GIRL:** Ah-ah-ah-ow-ow-oo! (*She stands, half rebellious, half bewildered.*)

36   **PICKERING:** (*very courteous*) Won't you sit down?

37   **LIZA:** (*coyly*) Don't mind if I do. (*She sits down.*)

38   **HIGGINS:** What's your name?

39   **THE FLOWER GIRL:** Liza Doolittle.

Pygmalion — Unit 4 • Transformation

Close Reading and Collaborative Conversations

What Does the Text Say?	How Does the Text Work?
1. What is this scene mostly about? Turn to a partner and summarize this excerpt from "Pygmalion."	1. How does the summary of Act 1 help the reader understand the excerpt from Act 2?
2. Why does Eliza want to improve the way she speaks?	2. In paragraph 3, Higgins is described as being "careless about . . . other people, including their feelings." How has the playwright shown this?
3. Who is Mrs. Pearce? What is her attitude toward Eliza?	3. Reread paragraphs 32–37. Why might the playwright have included these paragraphs?

Unit 4 • Transformation   Pygmalion

What Does the Text Mean?

1. How does the reader know that Professor Higgins and Eliza are from different social and financial classes? Why is that fact important to the story?

2. Later in the play, Professor Higgins agrees to teach Eliza how to speak better. Given that information and what you have read in the passage, why might the playwright have chosen the title "Pygmalion" for this play?

3. Compare reading this scene to watching a performance of this scene. Does it change your view of the characters and their actions? Explain why or why not.

Pygmalion — Unit 4 • Transformation

Write About the Text

Informative/Explanatory Writing Prompt

After reading "Pygmalion," write a paragraph describing one character for the actor who will be playing him or her. Include any acting suggestions or directions for how the character should be played. Support your description with evidence from the text.

Plan your response using this graphic organizer. Use your annotations and your notes on pages 100–105 to find text evidence.

Introduction:

Text Evidence:

Text Evidence:

Text Evidence:

Conclusion:

Writer's Checklist

- ❏ I introduced the topic.
- ❏ I clearly organized my ideas.
- ❏ I developed the topic with facts, details, and evidence.
- ❏ I used transitions to connect ideas.
- ❏ I used precise language.
- ❏ I used a formal style.
- ❏ I included a concluding statement.

Wrap Up
Check Your Understanding

1. This question has two parts. Read this sentence from paragraph 25 in the passage. Then, answer the questions. Answer Part A first, then answer Part B.

   > But they won't take me unless I can talk more genteel.

   Part A What is the meaning of genteel as used in this sentence?
   - A. knowledgeable
   - B. loud
   - C. quiet
   - D. proper

   Part B Which phrase from the passage helps you understand the meaning of genteel?
   - A. "What is it you want, my girl?"
   - B. "I want to be a lady in a flower shop 'stead of selling at the corner of Tottenham Court Road."
   - C. "Well, here I am ready to pay him—not asking any favor—and he treats me as if I was dirt."
   - D. "How can you be such a foolish ignorant girl as to think you could afford to pay Mr. Higgins?"

2. Which characteristic best describes Pickering?
   - A. arrogant
   - B. timid
   - C. compassionate
   - D. funny

Wrap Up
Check Your Understanding

3. Which of the following are true statements about the passage? Choose all that apply.
   - ☐ The story takes place in current times.
   - ☐ Professor Higgins thinks very highly of his ability to teach proper speech.
   - ☐ Mrs. Pearce feels sorry for Eliza.
   - ☐ Eliza knows what she wants.
   - ☐ Professor Higgins thinks he is superior to Eliza.
   - ☐ Pickering thinks he should be the one to teach Eliza to speak better.
   - ☐ Someone told Eliza that Professor Higgins could teach her to speak better.

4. Which of the following statements are true about both "The Myth of Pygmalion" and the excerpt from the play "Pygmalion"? Choose all that apply.
   - ☐ They both have people pretending to be something they are not.
   - ☐ They both are examples of realistic fiction.
   - ☐ They both have someone or something that is transformed by someone else.
   - ☐ They both have someone or something that transforms them.
   - ☐ They both have main characters who are afraid to ask for what they really want.

Unit 4 • Transformation   Read and Write Across Texts

Read and Write Across Texts

Plan your response using this graphic organizer. Use your annotations and the notes you've taken on each passage to identify supporting evidence for your response.

Introduction:

Evidence from "The Myth of Pygmalion":

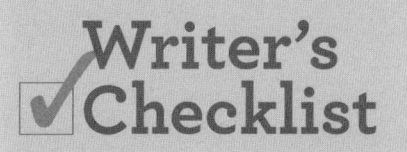

Informative/Explanatory Writing Prompt

After reading the three texts, write an essay that compares the different types of transformation portrayed in each of the texts. In discussing the play, you can also refer to the types of transformation that the characters want to happen but haven't happened yet. Support your discussion with evidence from the texts.

Writer's Checklist

- ❏ I introduced the topic.
- ❏ I developed the topic with facts, details, and evidence.
- ❏ I used transitions to connect ideas.
- ❏ I used precise language.
- ❏ I used a formal style.
- ❏ I included a concluding statement.

Evidence from "Operation Sherry":

Evidence from "Pygmalion":

Conclusion:

Unit 5
The Civil War

Table of Contents
The Great Emancipator. 112
O Captain! My Captain!. 118
The Civil War President 124

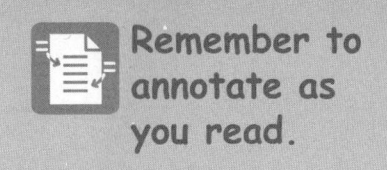

The Great Emancipator

by Harold Holzer

1. Nothing Abraham Lincoln ever did as president aroused so much celebration—and so much anger—as the Emancipation Proclamation. Even now, it remains one of the least understood and most controversial acts in U.S. history.

2. When it was issued in 1863, many white Americans were outraged, complaining bitterly that it changed the goal of the Civil War from saving the Union to freeing the slaves—a mission many people could not accept. However, some complaints today about the proclamation come not from whites but from African Americans, who contend that it accomplished nothing. They argue that the slaves freed themselves by fleeing from plantations on their own.

3. Lincoln's proclamation was a moral landmark. It also was a political stroke of genius that began the long-overdue process of crushing slavery.

4. To some, it may seem to have offered too little, too late, as it was not issued until the war was nearly two years old and at first it freed slaves only in states over which Lincoln had no control. But Lincoln knew he could not issue his revolutionary document until a majority of white Northerners were prepared to accept it and until he was sure it would not drive still-loyal slave states like Maryland into the Confederacy. As for limiting its reach, Lincoln had no legal authority to free slaves in Union states. Instead, the order was based on the commander in chief's power to seize the property of those in rebellion. Unquestionably, the slaves themselves had to accomplish with their feet what Lincoln had begun with his pen.

5   Newspapers and politicians the world over attacked Lincoln for daring to free the slaves. More Union soldiers than ever began deserting because of the proclamation. Many times in the months to come, advisers urged Lincoln to cancel his proclamation, but he steadfastly refused.

6   Lincoln knew that his order had only begun the work of ending slavery. "The harpoon is in the monster," he said. Now the monster had to be destroyed. To do this, Lincoln encouraged passage of the Thirteenth Amendment to the U.S. Constitution, outlawing slavery everywhere. Despite its passage, if Lincoln were alive today, he would likely be the first to admit that the work of ending slavery still remains unfinished.

7   Unfortunately, it has become fashionable to question Lincoln's commitment to the destruction of slavery. In reality, Lincoln truly deserved the title that a grateful America bestowed on him in 1863: "Great Emancipator."

Abraham Lincoln signed the final Emancipation Proclamation on January 1, 1863, freeing the slaves in all the states of the Confederacy.

The Great Emancipator | Unit 5 • The Civil War

Close Reading and Collaborative Conversations

What Does the Text Say?	How Does the Text Work?
1. What is this passage mostly about? Turn to a partner and summarize "The Great Emancipator."	**1.** What words does the author use to describe Lincoln's actions? What does the author's descriptive language reveal about the author's point of view?
2. Why were white Americans "outraged" by the Emancipation Proclamation? What examples does the author use to support the idea that people were outraged?	**2.** What is the author's point of view on the idea that the Emancipation Proclamation was "too little, too late"? How does the author support his point of view?
3. Why did some people believe the Emancipation Proclamation was "too little, too late"?	**3.** What does the author mean by the statement: "Unquestionably, the slaves themselves had to accomplish with their feet what Lincoln had begun with his pen"? What is the author's purpose for including this statement?

What Does the Text Mean?

1. What inferences can you make about the problem of slavery from Lincoln's statement that "the harpoon is in the monster"? What details in the text support your inferences?

2. What does the author mean in paragraph 6 when he states that if Lincoln were alive today, he would "admit that the work of ending slavery still remains unfinished"? How does this connect to the author's overall argument in the text?

3. Does the author provide enough evidence in the text to support his claim in paragraph 7 that Lincoln deserves the title "Great Emancipator"? Why or why not? Use details from the text to support your answer.

The Great Emancipator   Unit 5 • The Civil War

Write About the Text

Informative/Explanatory Writing Prompt

After reading "The Great Emancipator," write an essay explaining why the Emancipation Proclamation was a controversial act. Support your discussion with evidence from the text.

Writer's Checklist

- ❏ I clearly introduce the topic and preview what is in the essay.
- ❏ I use facts, details, and quotations from the text to develop my ideas.
- ❏ I use transitions to connect ideas and to explain relationships among ideas.
- ❏ I use precise language.
- ❏ I have a concluding paragraph that follows from and supports the information in the essay.

Plan your response using this graphic organizer. Use your annotations and your notes on pages 112–115 to find text evidence for your essay.

Introduction:

Reason 1:	Evidence:
Reason 2:	Evidence:
Reason 3:	Evidence:

Conclusion:

116   Accessing Complex Texts Now! • Grade 8 • © Benchmark Education Company, LLC

Wrap Up
Check Your Understanding

1. Which of the following statements would the author most likely agree with?

    A. Presidents have to consider many factors and outcomes when they are making a difficult decision.

    B. Presidents should always act immediately to correct an unfair law.

    C. People should never criticize any decisions made by the president.

    D. Presidents have limited power to make changes.

2. This question has two parts. Answer Part A first, then answer Part B.

    Part A Why was the passage of the Thirteenth Amendment necessary?

    A. to stop the criticism Lincoln received after signing the Emancipation Proclamation

    B. to end slavery everywhere in the United States

    C. to end slavery in the Confederate states

    D. because the Emancipation Proclamation was very controversial

    Part B Choose the sentences from the text that support your answer to Part A.

    ☐ "Newspapers and politicians the world over attacked Lincoln for daring to free the slaves."

    ☐ "To do this, Lincoln encouraged passage of the Thirteenth Amendment of the U.S. Constitution, outlawing slavery everywhere."

    ☐ "Even now, it remains one of the least understood and most controversial acts in U.S. history."

    ☐ "As for limiting its reach, Lincoln had no legal authority to free slaves in Union states."

    ☐ "Many times in the months to come, advisers urged Lincoln to cancel his proclamation, but he steadfastly refused."

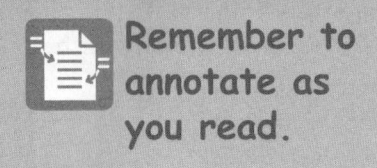

O Captain! My Captain!

by Walt Whitman

1 O Captain! my Captain! our fearful trip is done,
The ship has weather'd every rack, the prize we sought is won,
The port is near, the bells I hear, the people all exulting,
While follow eyes the steady keel, the vessel grim and daring;
5   But O heart! heart! heart!
        O the bleeding drops of red,
            Where on the deck my Captain lies,
                Fallen cold and dead.

O Captain! my Captain! rise up and hear the bells;
10 Rise up—for you the flag is flung—for you the bugle trills,
For you bouquets and ribbon'd wreaths—for you the shores a-crowding,
For you they call, the swaying mass, their eager faces turning;
        Here Captain! dear father!
            The arm beneath your head!
15   It is some dream that on the deck,
                You've fallen cold and dead.

My Captain does not answer, his lips are pale and still,
My father does not feel my arm, he has no pulse nor will,
The ship is anchor'd safe and sound, its voyage closed and done,
20 From fearful trip the victor ship comes in with object won;
        Exult O shores, and ring O bells!
            But I with mournful tread,
                Walk the deck my Captain lies,
                    Fallen cold and dead.

Unit 5 • The Civil War

O Captain! My Captain!

Notes

The funeral procession for President Abraham Lincoln passes down a city street in April 1865.

About the Author

Walt Whitman (1819–1892) was an American essayist, poet, and journalist. During the Civil War, he wrote *Drum-Taps*, a collection of poems about the war. After the assassination of Abraham Lincoln, Whitman wrote "O Captain! My Captain!" as a tribute to Lincoln and included it in *Sequel to Drum-Taps* and in later editions of *Leaves of Grass*.

O Captain! My Captain! Unit 5 • The Civil War

Close Reading and Collaborative Conversations

What Does the Text Say?	How Does the Text Work?
1. What is the poem mostly about? Turn to a partner and summarize "O Captain! My Captain!"	**1.** What phrases does the poet repeat? How does the poet vary the phrases throughout the poem? What effect does it have on the poem's mood and meaning?
2. Who is the speaker in the poem? Use details from the poem to support your answer.	**2.** In stanzas 2 and 3, the poet also refers to the captain as "dear father" and "my father." What does the word *father* reveal about the speaker's feelings? How is it different from the word *captain*?
3. Reread the final four lines of the poem. What is the meaning of these lines?	**3.** What contrasting images does Whitman use in each stanza? How do the images contribute to the poem's meaning?

What Does the Text Mean?

1. What is Whitman comparing to a voyage? What inferences can you make from Whitman's descriptions of the voyage?

2. Based on the poem, what can you infer about how people felt about Lincoln? Use details from the poem to support your answer.

3. Whitman wrote this poem as an elegy for Abraham Lincoln. Do you think the poem has meaning beyond honoring Abraham Lincoln? Why or why not?

O Captain! My Captain! Unit 5 • The Civil War

Write About the Text

Informative/Explanatory Writing Prompt

After reading "O Captain! My Captain!," write an essay in which you identify and explain the meaning of the central metaphor in the poem. Support your discussion with evidence from the text.

Plan your response using this graphic organizer. Use your annotations and your notes on pages 118-121 to find text evidence for your essay.

Introduction:

Text Evidence:

Text Evidence:

Text Evidence:

Conclusion:

Writer's Checklist

- ❏ I clearly introduce the topic and preview what is in the essay.
- ❏ I use facts, details, and quotations from the text to develop my ideas.
- ❏ I use transitions to connect ideas and to explain relationships among ideas.
- ❏ I use precise language.
- ❏ I have a concluding paragraph that follows from and supports the information in the essay.

Wrap Up
Check Your Understanding

1. This question has two parts. Answer Part A first, then answer Part B.

   Part A What is the mood of the crowd waiting on the shore?

   A. joyful and celebratory

   B. angry and protesting

   C. mournful and sad

   D. anxious and fearful

   Part B Which phrase from the poem best supports the answer to Part A?

   A. "the vessel grim and daring"

   B. "O the bleeding drops of red"

   C. "the bells I hear, the people all exulting"

   D. "the prize we sought is won"

2. What is the significance of the author's repeated use of the phrase "fallen cold and dead"?

   A. It is part of the rhyme scheme in the poem.

   B. It dramatically emphasizes the captain's death.

   C. It creates a sense of rhythm in the poem.

   D. It surprises the reader.

Passage 3 — Unit 5 • The Civil War

The Civil War President
by Harold Holzer

1   When Abraham Lincoln left his home in Illinois to begin the long journey to his inauguration as president, he told his neighbors he faced a task "greater than that which rested upon Washington." It was one of the most accurate predictions he ever made. No U.S. president before or after faced a graver crisis or emerged with a greater reputation.

2   Lincoln took his oath of office on March 4, 1861, assuring Southerners they had "no quarrel" with him. But quarrel they did. Southern states had already seceded and formed the Confederate States of America, presenting the most severe challenge to national authority in the country's brief history. Then in April, when Confederate forces opened fire on Fort Sumter, South Carolina, Lincoln promptly called for volunteers to defend the Union. The Civil War had begun.

3   In a special Independence Day message to Congress in 1861, Lincoln called the struggle ahead "a people's contest." He was determined to preserve majority rule, warning that if democracy was defeated in America, it would surely never rise again anywhere in the world.

4   Words alone did not win victories. Just weeks later, Union forces were crushed at the Battle of Bull Run. A despairing Lincoln realized that the struggle would be long, costly, and bloody. But he steadfastly rejected suggestions that he abandon the war and allow the South to leave the Union in peace.

5   Union impatience was understandable. The North boasted more men and better technology. The South claimed a brilliant corps of generals, including Robert E. Lee, whom Lincoln had tried to recruit to head the Union army. The Union lost again at the Second Battle of Bull Run (August 1862) and the Battle of Fredericksburg (December 1862). Union forces failed to capture the Confederate capital of Richmond after a long campaign in Virginia.

6   In September 1862, General Lee, fearing that Southern supplies would eventually run out, invaded Maryland. There Union forces finally triumphed at the Battle of Antietam. It was the bloodiest single day in the history of American warfare. Lincoln seized on the victory to issue the Emancipation Proclamation. He clearly hoped it would change the course of the war by threatening Southern productivity. Slaves still worked on farms and plantations while white men fought in the Confederate army.

7   Lincoln defended his momentous decision by declaring, "We cannot escape history." Although the emancipation certainly did change history, it did not immediately change the course of the war. In May 1863, Lee handed the Union one of its worst defeats at the Battle of Chancellorsville.

8   Meanwhile, many antiwar Northerners were demanding peace and openly urging disloyalty to the Union. Lincoln created more controversy by allowing military arrests of civilians and prolonged confinement of suspects awaiting trial. The government defended both as attempts to crack down on treason.

9   Lincoln also ordered America's first military draft. It was a highly unpopular, badly conceived system in which wealthy men could buy their way out of service. In July 1863, New York City erupted in riots triggered by the draft. Mobs lynched innocent blacks and even burned an orphanage for black children.

10   Earlier in July, the North won a major victory at the Battle of Gettysburg and captured Vicksburg, Mississippi, the same week. But as 1863 drew to a close, Lincoln probably ranked as the most unpopular president in history.

11   That November, Lincoln did with words what he had been unable to do with bullets. In a two-minute speech at Gettysburg, he rallied the North to what he called a "new birth of freedom" for America, vowing that government "of the people, by the people, for the people" would not "perish from the earth." It remains the greatest presidential speech ever given.

12   Lincoln also assumed an increasingly active role as commander in chief. It took him years to find the right generals. He hired and fired them with shocking swiftness in 1861 and 1862. But eventually he found reliable leaders such as Ulysses S. Grant and William T. Sherman.

13   In 1864, Lincoln made two major decisions, the importance of which is often overlooked. First, he allowed the presidential election to proceed as scheduled—something unheard of in countries torn by rebellion. In addition, Lincoln decided to run again for the presidency. No president since Andrew Jackson had been reelected to a second term.

Notes

14   The 1864 campaign was one of the ugliest in U.S. history. Lincoln was challenged by one of his former generals, George B. McClellan. McClellan's backers accused Lincoln of supporting intermarriage between blacks and whites, a ploy designed to panic voters.

15   Until the last few weeks of the campaign, Lincoln believed that he would lose the election. He even asked his own cabinet to sign, sight unseen, a pledge to cooperate with the next president. And he secretly plotted with black leader Frederick Douglass to spread news of emancipation in the South to encourage slaves to flee before the next president could overturn the order.

16   Two months before Election Day, Union forces captured Atlanta, turning the tide of the war. Lincoln went on to defeat McClellan, winning 55 percent of the popular vote and 212 of 233 electoral votes.

17   Lincoln's finest moment may have come at his second inaugural on March 4, 1865. He defended the sacrifice of lives that had been necessary to rid America of the evil of slavery and called for an era of "malice toward none" and "charity for all" to "bind up the nation's wounds" and create "lasting peace among ourselves."

18   The war ended a month later, and Lincoln began working on plans to reconstruct the devastated Union. He even hinted publicly that he would extend the right to vote to those black Americans who had fought to preserve the Union.

19   One of those who heard Lincoln offer that hope was an actor named John Wilkes Booth. An embittered Confederate sympathizer, Booth and several other conspirators fatally shot Lincoln at Ford's Theatre in Washington on Good Friday, April 14, 1865. Nine hours later, Lincoln died in a boarding house across the street.

20   A man may have died, but a legend was quickly born. Hated by many while he lived, Lincoln was now universally celebrated as a latter-day Moses who had led black Americans to freedom and a beloved martyr who had died at the moment of his greatest triumph. More than ever, he seemed to symbolize American opportunity. As Lincoln put it, if he could rise from log cabin to White House, "any man's son" could hope to do the same.

About the Author
Harold Holzer is a noted Lincoln scholar. He is the author and editor of more than thirty books on Lincoln, including *Lincoln: How Abraham Lincoln Ended Slavery in America, 1863: Lincoln's Pivotal Year,* and *Emancipating Lincoln: The Proclamation in Text, Context, and Memory.*

The Civil War President | Unit 5 • The Civil War

Close Reading and Collaborative Conversations

What Does the Text Say?	How Does the Text Work?
1. What is this passage mostly about? Turn to a partner and summarize "The Civil War President."	**1.** How does the author organize "The Civil War President"? Use details from the text to support your answer.
2. Why did Lincoln believe that the Emancipation Proclamation would improve the North's chances in the war?	**2.** In paragraph 11, what does the author mean when he states that "Lincoln did with words what he had been unable to do with bullets"? What does the statement reveal about the author's point of view?
3. Why was Lincoln so unpopular by the end of 1863? Use details from the text to support your answer.	**3.** What was the author's purpose in including the information in paragraph 15? How does it reflect the author's point of view?

What Does the Text Mean?

1. Lincoln said that he faced a task "greater than that which rested upon Washington." What did Lincoln mean by this statement? Which details in the text support this idea?

2. What inferences can you make about Lincoln from his decision to hold the presidential elections in 1864? What other details from the text support your response?

3. How does listening to the Gettysburg Address help you better understand and evaluate the claims the author makes in paragraph 11?

The Civil War President   Unit 5 • The Civil War

Write About the Text

Argument Writing Prompt

The author states that Lincoln's finest moment may have been at his second inaugural. After reading "The Civil War President," write an essay in which you address the question of Lincoln's greatest moment and argue what you believe it was. Support your position with details from the text.

Writer's Checklist

- ❏ I clearly introduce my claim.
- ❏ I acknowledge alternative or opposing claims.
- ❏ I support my claim with logical reasoning and relevant evidence.
- ❏ I use words, phrases, and clauses to create cohesion and to clarify relationships between ideas.
- ❏ I include a concluding statement that supports the argument that is presented.

Plan your response using this graphic organizer. Use your annotations and your notes on pages 124-131 to find text evidence for your essay.

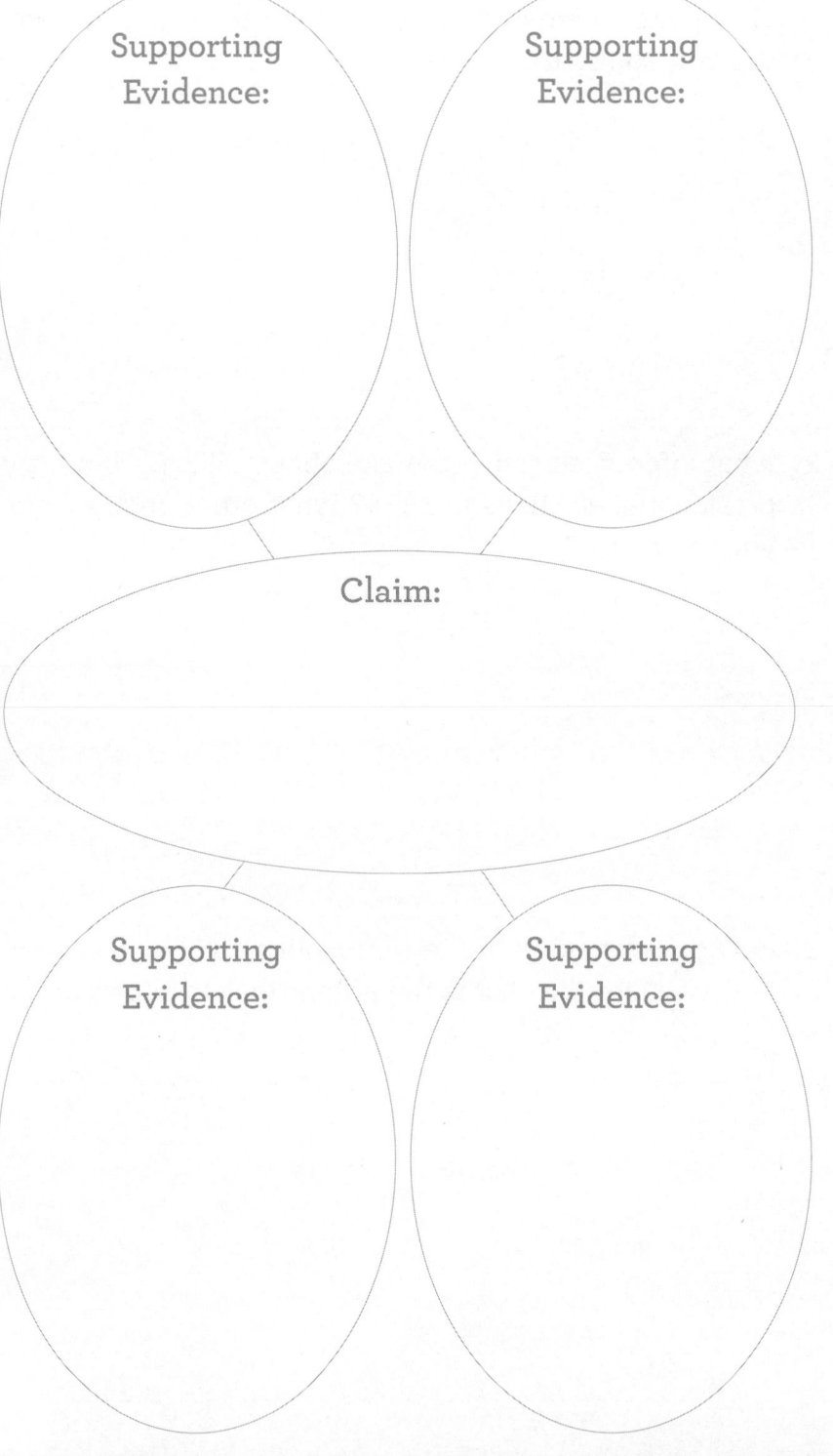

Supporting Evidence:

Supporting Evidence:

Claim:

Supporting Evidence:

Supporting Evidence:

Wrap Up
Check Your Understanding

1. Which of the following details support the idea that the war was not popular in the North? Select all the answers that apply.

    A. In July 1863, New York City erupted in riots triggered by the draft.

    B. The North boasted more men and better technology.

    C. Union forces failed to capture the Confederate capital of Richmond after a long campaign in Virginia.

    D. But as 1863 drew to a close, Lincoln probably ranked as the most unpopular president in history.

    E. In a two-minute speech at Gettysburg, he rallied the North to what he called a "new birth of freedom for America. . . ."

2. Based on Lincoln's remarks at his second inaugural, what inference can be made?

    A. Lincoln wanted to punish the South for the war.

    B. Lincoln regretted the results of the war.

    C. Lincoln wanted to promote forgiveness between the North and South.

    D. Lincoln did not think that the war was going to end soon.

3. Which of the following does the author suggest was a motive for John Wilkes Booth's assassination of Lincoln?

    A. the reelection of Lincoln

    B. Lincoln's plan to extend the right to vote to black Americans

    C. the end of the Civil War

    D. the remarks Lincoln made at his second inaugural

Wrap Up
Check Your Understanding

4. Which of the following statements would the author most likely agree with?

    A. It was clear that the Union was going to win the war from the beginning.

    B. Lincoln's most important decisions was selecting Ulysses S. Grant and William T. Sherman.

    C. It was wrong for people in the North to protest the war.

    D. To win the war, Lincoln had to make unpopular decisions.

5. Read the following sentenced from the passage.

    > Two months before Election Day, Union forces captured Atlanta, turning the tide of the war.

    Which of the following best matches the meaning of turning the tide in the sentence above?

    A. changing the direction

    B. improving the situation

    C. securing the victory

    D. stopping the flow

Unit 5 • The Civil War

Read and Write Across Texts

Plan your essay using this graphic organizer. Use your annotations and the notes you've taken on each passage to identify supporting evidence for your essay.

Introduction:

Evidence from "The Great Emancipator":

Argument Writing Prompt

In "The Civil War President," the author states that "a legend was quickly born" after Lincoln's death. What traits make Lincoln a legend? After reading the three passages, write an essay addressing this question. Support your position with examples from the texts.

Writer's Checklist

- ❏ I clearly introduced my claim.
- ❏ I cited alternative or opposing claims.
- ❏ I supported my claim with logical reasoning and relevant evidence.
- ❏ I used words, phrases, and clauses to create cohesion and to clarify relationships between ideas.
- ❏ I included a concluding statement that supports the argument presented.

Read and Write Across Texts — Unit 5 • The Civil War

Evidence from "O Captain! My Captain!":

Evidence from 'The Civil War President":

Conclusion:

Unit 6
Space Frontiers

Table of Contents
The Voyager Mission 138
Great Achievements in Planetary Exploration . 144
The Search for Another Earth 152

Passage 1 — Unit 6 • Space Frontiers

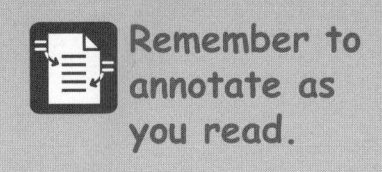

The Voyager Mission

1   The twin spacecrafts Voyager 1 and Voyager 2 were launched by NASA in the summer of 1977 from Cape Canaveral, Fla. The Voyagers were designed to conduct close-up studies of Jupiter and Saturn, Saturn's rings, and the larger moons of the two planets. Now, more than 35 years later, they have explored four planets between them. And in August 2012, Voyager 1 left the solar system. It is the first human-made object to travel that far into space.

2   The Voyager mission was designed to take advantage of a rare arrangement of the outer planets in the late 1970s and 1980s. This layout of Jupiter, Saturn, Uranus and Neptune occurs about every 175 years. It allows a spacecraft on a particular flight path to swing from one planet to the next without the need for large onboard propulsion systems. The flyby of each planet bends the spacecraft's flight path and increases its velocity enough to deliver it to the next destination. Using this "gravity assist" technique, the flight time to Neptune was reduced from 30 years to 12.

3   Voyager 1 reached Jupiter in 1979 and Saturn in 1980. Voyager 2 flew by Jupiter in 1979 and Saturn in 1981. Voyager 1's trajectory was designed to send it closely past the large moon Titan and behind Saturn's rings.

4   After Voyager 2's successful Saturn encounter, it flew on to Uranus. It encountered the planet on January 24, 1986. It returned detailed photos and other data on the planet, its moons, magnetic field and dark rings. It made its closest approach to Neptune on August 25, 1989. Then Voyager 2 flew over Neptune's north pole and went past Neptune's moon Triton, with an ultimate goal of departing our solar system.

Unit 6 • Space Frontiers   The Voyager Mission

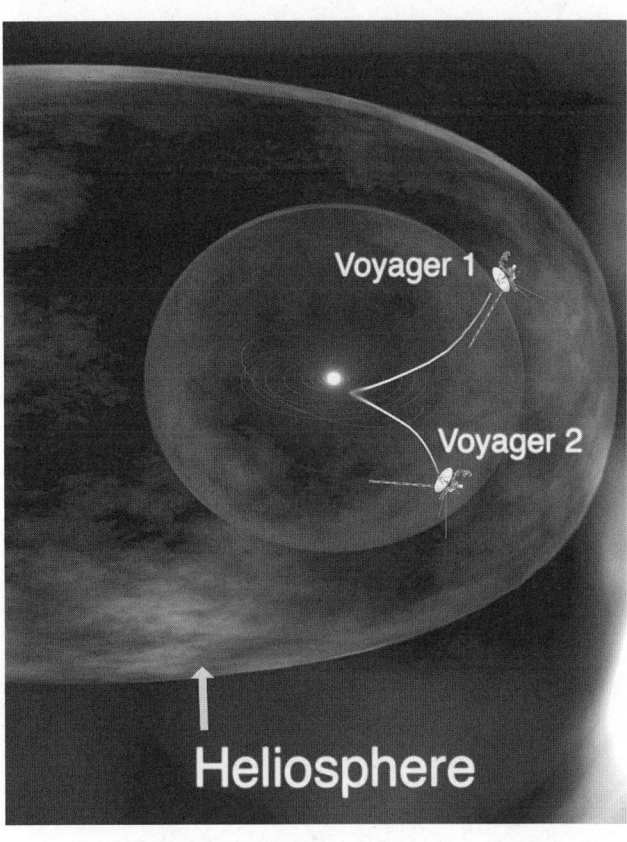

Voyager 1 had to travel through the heliopause, the transition area between our solar system and interstellar space.

Heliosphere

5   In January 1990, Voyager 1 began to journey to the edge of the solar system. In August of 2013, scientists were able to determine that it was traveling outside the heliosphere. The heliosphere is the bubble that contains our solar system. Scientists think that it passed boundary of our solar system and began traveling in interstellar space on August 25, 2012. Voyager 1 is now 11.7 billion miles away from Earth. Scientists expect that Voyager 2 will also leave the solar system.

6   The Voyagers are expected to return valuable data for at least another eight years. Communications will be maintained until the Voyagers' power sources can no longer supply enough energy. Until then, scientists gather as much information as they can.

Adapted from NASA Voyager Mission Overview

Notes

The Voyager Mission | Unit 6 • Space Frontiers

💬 Close Reading and Collaborative Conversations

What Does the Text Say?	How Does the Text Work?
1. What is a central idea of this article? What are two details that support the central idea?	**1.** What is the purpose of paragraph 2? What key concept does it introduce, and how does the last sentence refine that concept?
2. Why was it good for the mission that the spacecrafts were able to be launched in the 1970s?	**2.** In paragraph 2, what does the word "velocity" mean? What context clues help you determine its meaning?
3. What was the purpose of launching Voyager 1 and Voyager 2?	**3.** What is the purpose of this article? Use details from the text to support your answer.

Unit 6 • Space Frontiers

The Voyager Mission

What Does the Text Mean?

1. The text calls Voyager 2's mission to Saturn "successful." What qualifies the Voyager missions as successful or unsuccessful? Use evidence from the text.

2. Why is it notable that Voyager 1 has left the heliosphere? What are likely effects of this event? Include evidence from the text.

3. In paragraph 5, the author uses phrases like "scientists were able to determine," "scientists think," and "scientists expect." Why might the author do this?

The Voyager Mission   Unit 6 • Space Frontiers

Write About the Text

Informative/Explanatory Writing Prompt

After reading "The Voyager Mission," write an essay explaining the main purpose of the mission. What goals did the people who designed the mission have in mind? How has the mission met those goals? Support your discussion with evidence from the text.

Plan your response using this graphic organizer. Use your annotations and your notes on pages 138–141 to find evidence for your essay.

Topic:

Detail:

Explain:

Detail:

Explain:

Conclusion:

Writer's Checklist

- ❏ I introduced the topic.
- ❏ I clearly organized my ideas.
- ❏ I developed the topic with facts, details, and evidence.
- ❏ I used transitions to connect ideas.
- ❏ I used precise language.
- ❏ I used a formal style.
- ❏ I included a concluding statement.

Wrap Up
Check Your Understanding

1. What does the phrase gravity assist mean as used in the paragraph 2?

   A. The journeys of the spacecrafts were assisted by the gravitational pull of the planets they were passing.

   B. The gravity of the spacecrafts assisted them in their mission to document the planets they were passing.

   C. The scientists used a gravity machine to create power to help move the spacecrafts.

   D. The gravitational pull of the sun assisted the spacecrafts in their mission.

2. This question has two parts. Answer Part A first. Then answer Part B.

   Part A In paragraph 3, what does the word trajectory mean?

   A. path

   B. gravity

   C. engine

   D. cameras

   Part B What evidence in the text supports the answer you chose?

   A. "large moon Titan"

   B. "send it closely past"

   C. "behind Saturn's rings"

   D. "reached Jupiter in 1979"

Passage 2

Unit 6 • Space Frontiers

Great Achievements in Planetary Exploration

Michelle Thaller is an American astronomer and research scientist. She is the Director for Science Communication at NASA's Goddard Space Center. In the following passage, Ms. Thaller shares what she thinks are most significant events in planetary exploration.

1   I would have to put the Voyagers first on my list. The Voyagers completely changed the way we view the outer solar system. Through Voyager we were able to see what Jupiter's moons looked like, what Saturn looked like from the other side and so much more. No longer were the outer planets and their moons just fuzzy little blobs in the sky, but actual places we could imagine being.

Voyager I was launched into space on September 5, 1977.

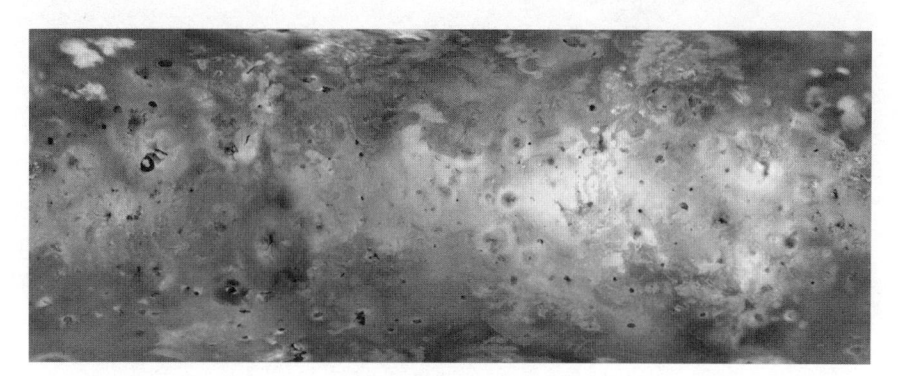

Unit 6 • Space Frontiers   Great Achievements in Planetary Exploration

Voyager took the first photographs of the surface of Jupiter's moon, Io.

2   The most surprising moon visited by Voyager was Jupiter's moon Io, the innermost of the four Galilean moons. We had no idea that we could have a moon similar in size to our own Moon that had two to three hundred active volcanoes going off on it all the time. We only flew past Io a few times during the Voyager encounters, but every time we did fly by there were hundreds of volcanoes erupting on this moon.

3   The finding of volcanism on Io really changed our idea of what a habitable zone means in the solar system. We thought that the outer solar system was cold, icy and dead. We also thought that a planet or moon could only have liquid water or sufficient warmth if it was "snuggled up" close to a star. However, we found moons that run on tidal energy rather than sunlight in the outer solar system. In the case of Europa, this could mean that there may be life just underneath the ice.

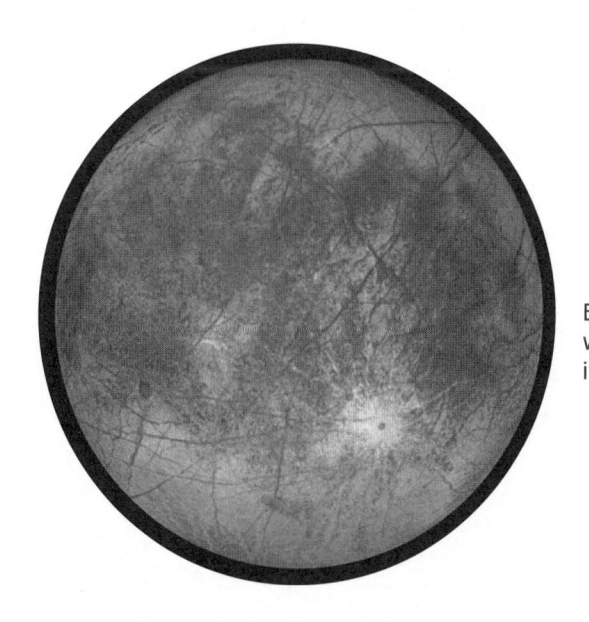

Europa uses tidal energy, which is energy it gets from its orbit around Jupiter.

Notes

145

Passage 2 *continued*

Unit 6 • Space Frontiers

4   Titan, with its thick atmosphere, is a place where it is literally raining organic molecules all the time—imagine being knee deep in organics. Titan is really so organic-rich, we have to wonder: "Could there be a life system based on methane rather than water?" "Or, in fact, is there water underneath the methane?"

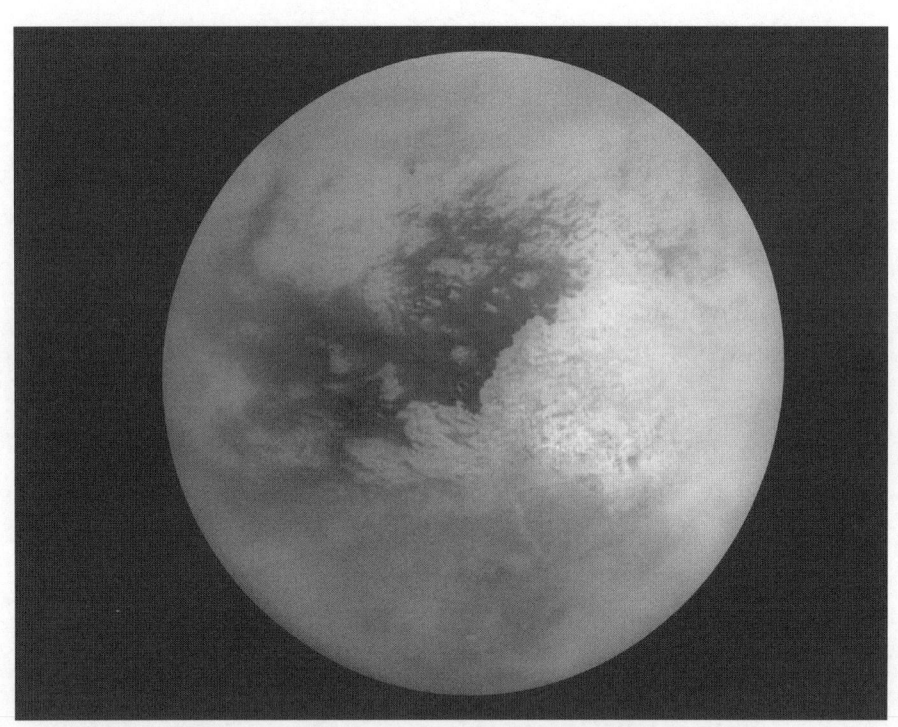

Scientists were able to determine the size of Saturn's moon Titan with data collected by the Voyager mission.

5   I am sometimes disappointed by how so few of the public know that we landed on Titan. We actually parachuted through the atmosphere of Titan and landed on the surface near a giant methane lake. We saw methane rivers, and it was raining as the probe fell down. It is absolutely incredible that there is a little spacecraft on Titan right now!

6   When I was a child, life somewhere else in our solar system seemed really unlikely, at least no one was talking about it seriously. Now we can ask the question: "Which of the places shall we explore first?" There may be life in half a dozen places in our solar system.

7   In regards to evidence for life in our Universe: Recently, I was speaking with Jason Dworkin (head of astrobiology at Goddard). He showed me some of the aerogel, or porous solid, from the Stardust mission that had picked up samples from comet Wild 2. From this comet dust, they are isolating little bits of DNA—amino acids. Scientists are finding the building blocks of life in these comet samples. It was strange to be sitting in a room with something on the table that had flown through a comet's tail and returned a sample to Earth. It is just mind blowing to think that we have that sort of a connection to our local Universe.

8   The same is true of Saturn's moon Enceladus. Unlike Europa, there is not a doubt that there is water on Enceladus. We know that each day, as the tides go by, the cracks on Enceladus open and shut and water gushes out. This evidence, and the evidence at Europa, supports the theory of possible life habitats in the outer solar system. No one had expected this before the missions to the outer planets.

9   I very often look at the pictures of Mars that are coming back from the Mars Reconnaissance Orbiter (MRO) and from the rovers. I enjoy watching the little movie of the dust devils—the little tornadoes turning around on the deserts of Mars. When I look at that great little video I think: "That is Mars! That is Mars where those tornadoes are and here I am watching them!"

Great Achievements in Planetary Exploration   Unit 6 • Space Frontiers

🗨️ Close Reading and Collaborative Conversations

What Does the Text Say?	How Does the Text Work?
1. What are two specific achievements in planetary exploration that Thaller mentions?	**1.** What is the purpose of this text, and how does the way the author writes it reveal its purpose?
2. What in particular impressed Thaller about the landing on Titan?	**2.** How does the author's use of first person pronouns such as "I" and "we" affect the tone of this piece?
3. What idea, stated in paragraph 8, does Thaller say was not considered before the Voyager missions?	**3.** Why is Thaller "sometimes disappointed" by how little some people know about the landing on Titan? Explain her point of view.

What Does the Text Mean?

1. Both "Great Achievements in Planetary Exploration" and "The Voyager Mission" outline some of the notable accomplishments of the Voyager spacecrafts. Summarize the main difference in how each text addresses those accomplishments.

2. What does Thaller want the reader to come away from the article with, other than information about what she thinks are important achievements?

3. What message is Thallar trying to get across by writing, "It was strange to be sitting in a room with something on the table that had flown through a comet's tail..."?

Great Achievements in Planetary Exploration · Unit 6 • Space Frontiers

Write About the Text

Informative/Explanatory Writing Prompt

After reading "Great Achievements in Planetary Exploration," write an essay explaining the major new discoveries that have resulted from planetary exploration. Use evidence from the text to support your ideas.

Plan your response using this graphic organizer. Use your annotations and your notes on pages 144–149 to find evidence for your essay.

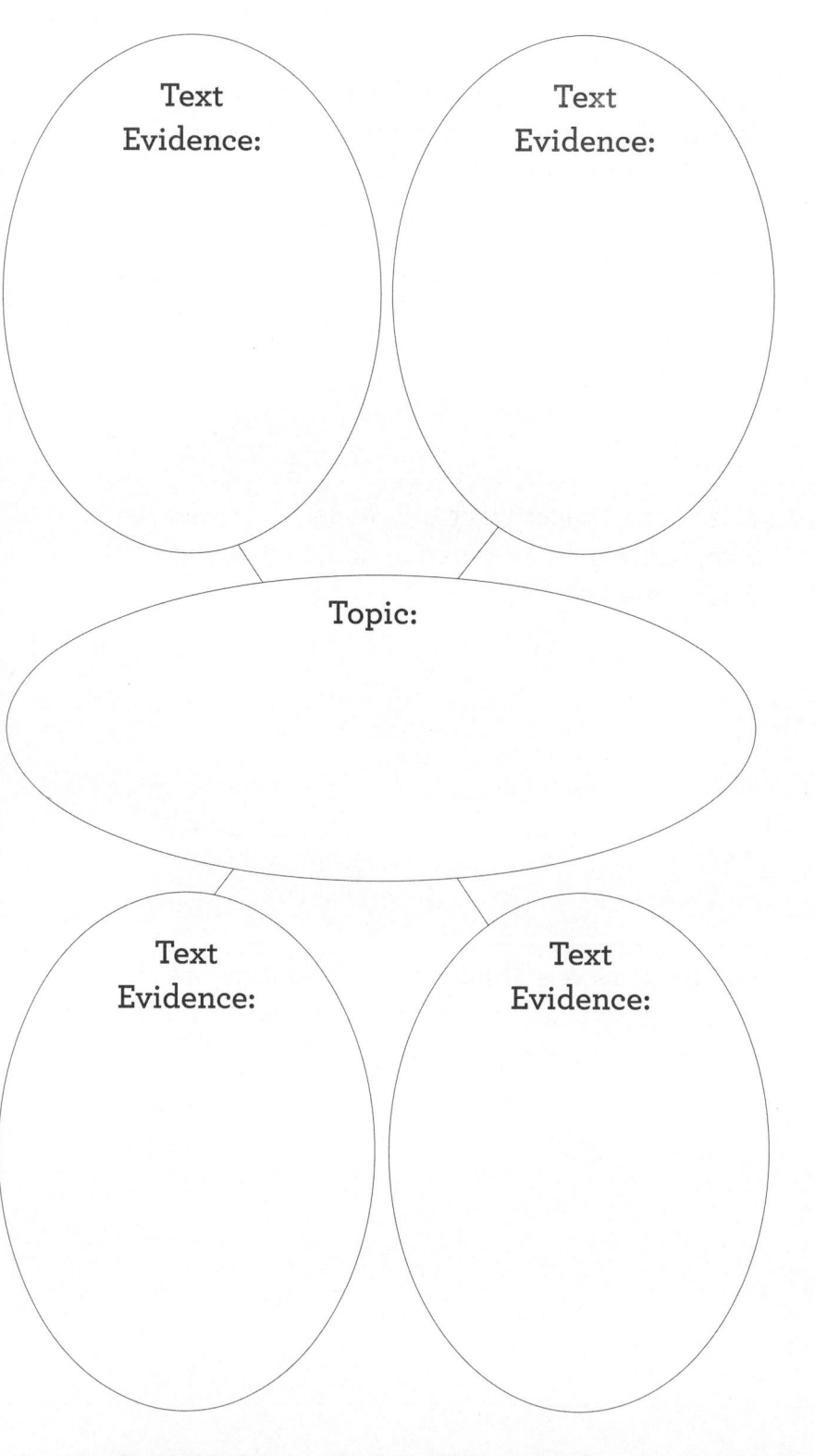

Writer's Checklist

- ❏ I introduced the topic.
- ❏ I clearly organized my ideas.
- ❏ I developed the topic with facts, details, and evidence.
- ❏ I used transitions to connect ideas.
- ❏ I used precise language.
- ❏ I used a formal style.
- ❏ I included a concluding statement.

Text Evidence:

Text Evidence:

Topic:

Text Evidence:

Text Evidence:

Wrap Up
Check Your Understanding

1. This is a two-part question. Answer Part A first, then answer Part B.

   Part A Pick two things that scientists believe are conducive to life in space.
   - ☐ liquid water
   - ☐ sufficient warmth
   - ☐ methane
   - ☐ volcanoes

   Part B What evidence from the text supports your answers?
   - A. "Could there be a life system based on methane rather than water?"
   - B. "…every time we did fly by there were hundreds of volcanoes erupting on this moon."
   - C. "We saw methane rivers, and it was raining as the probe fell down."
   - D. "We also thought that a planet or moon could only have liquid water or sufficient warmth if it was 'snuggled up' close to a star."

2. What statement would the author of this article agree with?
   - A. The public is very well informed about accomplishments in space.
   - B. It's not necessary for the public to be informed about space accomplishments.
   - C. Few people know or understand the major accomplishments achieved by humans in space.
   - D. The accomplishments of our space exploration teams have not been very impressive.

Passage 3 — Unit 6 • Space Frontiers

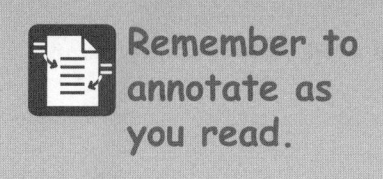

The Search for Another EARTH

1. Are we alone? Are their other planets like ours? Does life exist elsewhere in the universe?

2. These are questions mankind has been asking since the time of Greek philosophers. But for years, those answers have been elusive, if not impossible to find.

3. Today, astronomers are in hot pursuit of the first discovery of an Earth-like exoplanet. An exoplanet is a planet orbiting a star other than the sun. The discovery of one that resembles Earth could redefine our understanding of the universe and our place in it. It would be especially big if astronomers can also find signs that life exists on that planet's surface.

Exoplanet History

4. In 1584, when the Catholic monk Giordano Bruno asserted that there were "countless suns and countless earths all rotating around their suns," he was accused of heresy. But even in Bruno's time, the idea of many worlds wasn't entirely new. As far back as ancient Greece, humankind has speculated that other solar systems might exist. They've also speculated that some would harbor other forms of life. The Earth was dethroned as the center of the universe in early in the 16th century. That's when Copernicus discovered that our planet orbits the sun, instead of everything orbiting Earth. His insight, while reluctantly accepted, changed Western thinking forever.

Unit 6 • Space Frontiers   The Search for Another Earth

5   At the dawn of the 20th century, Edwin Hubble, using what was then the largest telescope in the world, found that the small nebulae in the sky were neighboring islands of stars far outside our own galaxy. Each one containing hundreds of billions of stars.

6   Hubble's observations proved that the potential for habitable planets are immeasurable. Still, almost an entire century went by without convincing proof of planets around even the nearest stars. On several occasions, discoveries of such planets were announced. But they were later found to be false.

Notes

Edwin Hubble studied the night sky from the Mount Wilson Observatory in California.

Passage 3 continued

Unit 6 • Space Frontiers

7   Because planets are too small and distant to be observed directly, astronomers have sought to discover their existence by detecting their effects on the host star. During the late 1960s, astronomer Peter van de Kamp claimed to have detected two planets near Barnard's Star using this technique. Barnard's Star is the second nearest star system to the sun. However, subsequent observations failed to verify the existence of either planet.

Pulsar's rotate, which is what makes them appear to pulse.

Scientists use radio telescopes like this one to study radio waves from stars and other objects in space.

Truly Alien Worlds

8   The first true extrasolar planet discovery came in 1994. Dr. Alexander Wolszczan, a radio astronomer at Pennsylvania State University, reported what he called "unambiguous proof" of extrasolar planetary systems.

9   While scientists accepted his assessment, those hoping for evidence of planetary systems similar to our own were disappointed. Wolszczan had discovered two or three planet-sized objects orbiting a pulsar, rather than a normal star. A pulsar is a dense, rapidly spinning remnant of a supernova explosion.

10   Wolszczan made his discovery by observing regular variations in the pulsar's rapidly pulsed radio signal This indicated the planets' complex gravitational effects on the dead star.

11   The origins of Wolszczan's unexpected pulsar planets remains a matter of debate, but there is little controversy on one point. These worlds couldn't support life as we know it. They would be permanently bathed in radiation. They would be barren and inhospitable.

An Onrush of Discovery

12   The first discovery of a planet orbiting a star similar to the sun came in 1995. The Swiss team of Michel Mayor and Didier Queloz of Geneva announced that they had found a rapidly orbiting world located blisteringly close to the star 51 Pegasi. Their planet was at least half the mass of Jupiter and no more than twice its mass.

13   These announcements marked the beginning of a flood of discoveries. Three months later, a team led by Geoffrey W. Marcy and Paul Butler of San Francisco State University and the University of California at Berkeley confirmed the Swiss discovery. They also turned up two more planets. By the end of the 20th century, several dozen worlds had been discovered, many the result of months or years of observation of nearby stars.

14   Astronomers attribute the abrupt surge in discoveries, in part, to technological advances in recent years. These include:

15   • Significant improvements in spectrometers, instruments that separate starlight into its component colors for analysis.

16   • Better electronic sensors that record the incoming starlight collected by telescope optics.

17   • The development of computer software that can reliably discern fluctuations in starlight and the motion induced by the gravitational pull of unseen companions.

18   Furthermore, the maturation of these technologies has led to intensified searches and data gathering.

Unit 6 • Space Frontiers　　　The Search for Another Earth

The Kepler space telescope has been an important tool in the search for exoplanets.

A New Era of Exploration

19　Now that exoplanet hunting is a mainstream part of astronomy, the race is on to build instruments that can find more and more planets. Astronomers are especially interested in worlds that could be like our own.

20　The French CoRoT mission, launched in 2006, was the first dedicated exoplanet space mission. It has contributed dozens of confirmed exoplanets to the ranks. It boasts a roster of some of the most well-studied planets outside our solar system.

21　NASA's first exoplanet mission, Kepler, launched in 2009, and has revolutionized how astronomers understand the universe and our place in it. It has made discoveries. Kepler has found that small planets are likely to be the most common in the galaxy. It has also found that our sun is an unusually calm star. Kepler has found exotic, multi-planet solar systems. As it continues its mission, it's likely that Kepler will find planets the size of our own that might in habitable areas.

22　Kepler may be NASA's first exoplanet mission, but it certainly won't be the last. Multiple technology initiatives at NASA are working on better ways to detect, characterize, and even directly image exoplanets, while searching for habitable worlds close to our own solar system

Notes

The Search for Another Earth   Unit 6 • Space Frontiers

🗨 Close Reading and Collaborative Conversations

What Does the Text Say?	How Does the Text Work?
1. What is the main idea of this passage? Turn to a partner and summarize "The Search for Another Earth."	1. What does the term "elusive" mean as used in the paragraph 2? Explain how context clues can help define the word.
2. What important discovery did Edwin Hubble make in the early 20th century?	2. What is the structure of paragraph 7? What two ideas is it introducing, and how does the structure show that one idea is subordinate to the other?
3. What did Dr. Wolszczan discover in 1994? Summarize the importance of his discovery.	3. What is the purpose of this text? Is the author trying to convince or explain? Give evidence to support your choice.

158   Accessing Complex Texts Now! • Grade 8 • © Benchmark Education Company, LLC

Unit 6 • Space Frontiers The Search for Another Earth

What Does the Text Mean?

1. Both "The Search for Another Earth" and "Great Achievements in Planetary Explorations" focus on the search for life in the universe outside of Earth. How is the information provided in these articles different?

2. In paragraph 6, the author states that "Hubble's observations proved that the potential for habitable planets are immeasurable." What evidence does the author provide to support this idea?

3. Based on what you have read in the selections in this unit, are we close to finding a new planet like Earth? Explain your reasoning and use details from the text to support your ideas.

© Benchmark Education Company, LLC • Grade 8 • Accessing Complex Texts Now!

The Search for Another Earth — Unit 6 • Space Frontiers

Write About the Text

Argument Writing Prompt

After reading "The Search for Another Earth," write an essay answering the question: Is the discovery of an exoplanet that supports life likely in the next few years, based on the trajectory of discovery described in this article? Support your opinion with evidence from the text.

Plan your response using this graphic organizer. Use your annotations and your notes on pages 152–159 to find evidence for your essay.

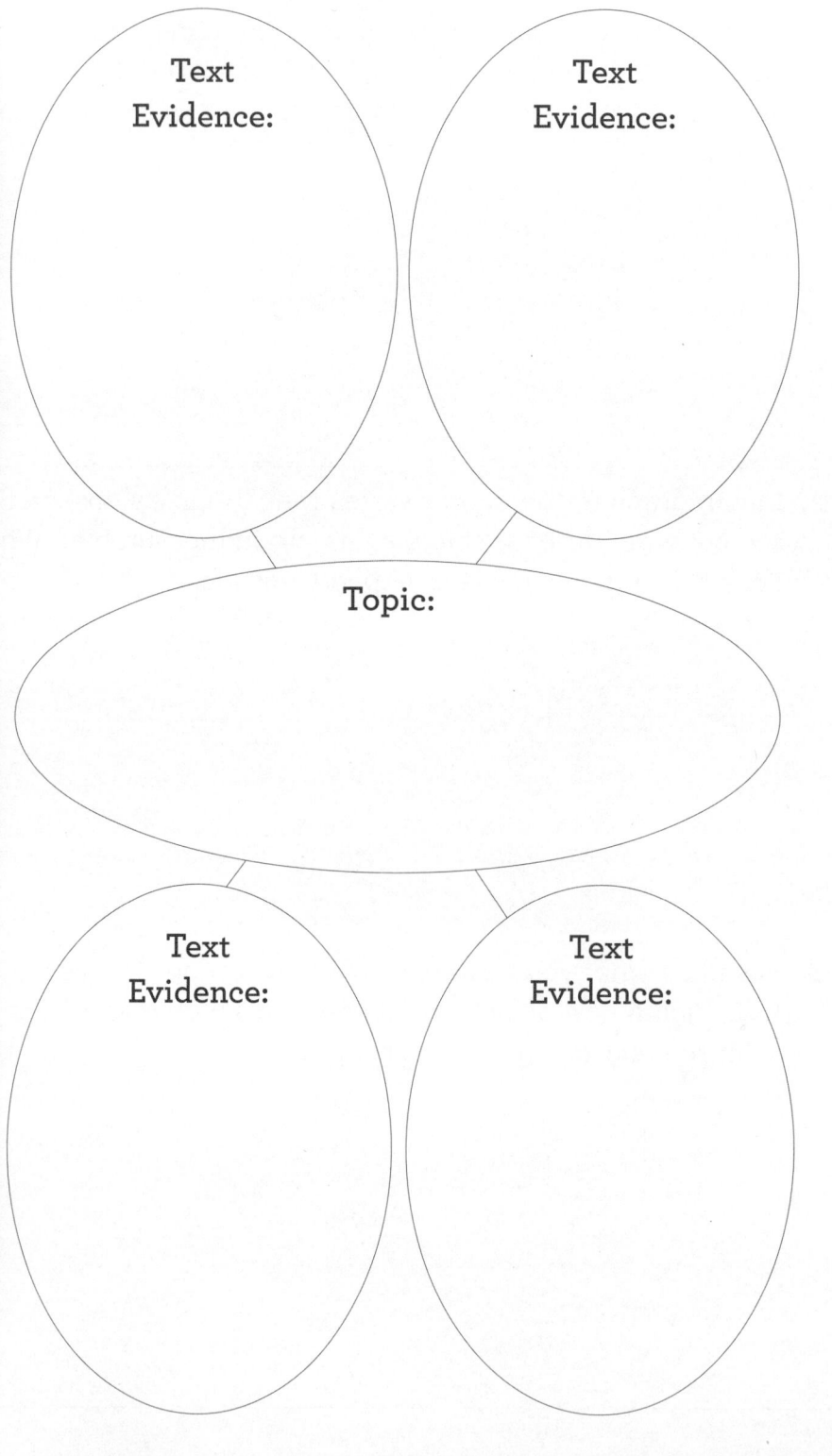

- Text Evidence:
- Text Evidence:
- Topic:
- Text Evidence:
- Text Evidence:

Writer's Checklist

- ❏ I introduced a claim.
- ❏ I acknowledged opposing claims.
- ❏ I supported my claim with evidence and logical reasoning.
- ❏ I used words and phrases to make connections and clarify idea.
- ❏ I used a formal style.
- ❏ I included a concluding statement.

Wrap Up
Check Your Understanding

1. Pick two statements that accurately describe the history of exoplanet research.

   ☐ The planet that Wolszczan discovered in 1994 is thought to possibly support life.

   ☐ Exoplanets were thought to exist long before evidence of their existence was recorded by instruments.

   ☐ With powerful telescopes, scientists can study the surfaces of far away exoplanets.

   ☐ More than 20 exoplanets have been discovered, based on observation of nearby stars.

   ☐ The planet discovered by Michael Mayor and Didier Queloz was discovered to be orbiting a pulsar.

2. Read the following sentence from the passage.

   > Furthermore, the maturation of these technologies had led to intensified searches and data gathering.

   Select the word that best defines maturation as it is used in the passage.

   A. growth

   B. development

   C. invention

   D. sophistication

Wrap Up
Check Your Understanding

3. This question has two parts. Answer Part A first. Then answer Part B.

    Part A In paragraph 11, what does the word <u>barren</u> mean?
    - A. controversial
    - B. unable to support life
    - C. pulsing
    - D. unfriendly

    Part B What evidence from the text best supports your answer?
    - A. "unexpected pulsar"
    - B. "there is little controversy on one point"
    - C. "couldn't support life as we know it"
    - D. "inhospitable"

4. Which of the following details explains why scientists have been able to find more exoplanets in recent years?
    - A. new technology that helps scientists study the universe
    - B. the launch of the French CoRot mission in 2006
    - C. Dr. Wolszczan's discovery of exoplanetary systems
    - D. the discovery of the planet near star 51 Pegasi

Unit 6 • Space Frontiers   **Read and Write Across Texts**

Read and Write Across Texts

Plan your essay using this graphic organizer. Use your annotations and the notes you've taken on each passage to identify supporting evidence for your essay.

Introduction:

Evidence from "The Voyager Mission":

Argument Writing Prompt

Each of these informational texts gives either information or opinion on recent space exploration. Write your own list of which three discoveries discussed in any of these articles are your "top three." Explain what is exceptionally interesting or important about each of the three you picked. Support your position with examples from the texts.

Writer's Checklist

- ❏ I introduced a claim.
- ❏ I acknowledged opposing claims.
- ❏ I supported my claim with evidence and logical reasoning.
- ❏ I used words and phrases to make connections and clarify idea.
- ❏ I used a formal style.
- ❏ I have a concluding statement.

Read and Write Across Texts

Unit 6 • Space Frontiers

Evidence from "Great Achievements in Planetary Exploration":

Evidence from "The Search for Another Earth":

Conclusion:

Notes

Notes

Notes

Notes

Notes

Notes

Notes

Notes

Notes

Notes

Notes

Acknowledgments

"Fancy Feather Gene" by Stephen Ornes, copyright (c) 2013 by Society for Science and the Public. Reprinted with permission.

"What's On Your Genes?" by Sharon Pochron, copyright (c) 2011 by Society for Science and the Public. Reprinted with permission.

"The Constitutional Convention Begins" adapted from the National Archives, http://www.archives.gov/exhibits/charters/constitution_history.html.

"January 1, 1863 The Great Emancipator" by Harold Holzer, from *Cobblestone* issue: Famous Dates, © 1995 Cobblestone Publishing Company, 30 Grove Street, Suite C, Peterborough, NH 03458. All Rights Reserved. Used by permission of the publisher. www.cobblestonepub.com.

"A Nation at War", by Harold Holzer, from *Cobblestone* issue: Lincoln: With Malice Toward None, © 2008 Cobblestone Publishing Company, 30 Grove Street, Suite C, Peterborough, NH 03458. All Rights Reserved. Used by permission of the publisher. www.cobblestonepub.com.

"Voyager Mission" courtesy of NASA Jet Propulsion Laboratory, http://voyager.jpl.nasa.gov/science/planetary.html.

"Great Achievements in Planetary Exploration" Courtesy of NASA, http://solarsystem.nasa.gov/scitech/display.cfm?ST_ID=2471.

"The Search for Another Earth" courtesy of NASA, http://planetquest.jpl.nasa.gov/page/history.

Photo Credits:

Page 35: © Pictorial Press Ltd/Alamy; Page 36: © Image Asset Management Ltd./Alamy; Page 37: © Martin Shields/Alamy; Page 43: © PetStockBoys/Alamy; Page 49: Courtesy of Dr. Randy L. Jirtle; Pages 111A, 111B: Library of Congress; Page 119A: © Museum of the City of New York/Corbis; Page 126: The Granger Collection, NYC; Pages 137, 139, 144A, 144B, 145A, 145B, 146, 154, 155, 156: NASA; Page 153: © Bettmann/CORBIS

Illustration Credits
Little Women Playing Pilgrims Diane Le Feyer